THE SURREY STYLE

RODERICK GRADIDGE is an architect and architectural historian; an authority on Edwin Lutyens and the Arts and Crafts Movement, his professional work has included additions and alterations to houses by Lutyens and his contemporaries. He has written two books *Dream Houses – The Edwardian Ideal* (1980) a study of Arts and Crafts domestic architecture and *Edwin Lutyens – Architect Laureate* (1981); he is a regular contributor to *Country Life*.

THE SURREY HISTORIC BUILDINGS TRUST is a registered charity set up in 1980 with the aim of preserving historic buildings in the county. With initial capital subscribed by Surrey County Council and Philip Henman, a former High Sheriff, the Trust has wide powers to purchase, restore and sell buildings of historical and architectural importance in Surrey. The Trust also makes small grants for conservation and restoration of features and architectural details of individual houses and buildings.

THE SURREY HISTORIC BUILDINGS TRUST LTD.,
COUNTY HALL, KINGSTON UPON THAMES, SURREY

RODERICK GRADIDGE

THE SURREY STYLE

SURREY HISTORIC BUILDINGS TRUST
1991

© 1991 *The Surrey Historic Buildings Trust*

Text © 1991 *Roderick Gradidge*

Designed by Francis Graham

Printed by Craddocks of Godalming

CONTENTS

PART I

one	THE MAKING OF THE SURREY STYLE	7
two	HOW & HOW NOT TO ADD TO AN OLD BUILDING	17
three	MAKING ADDITIONS TO OLDER BUILDINGS	23
four	ADDITIONS BY ARCHITECTS WORKING IN THE VERNACULAR TRADITION	37
five	THE NEW SURREY STYLE	51
six	ADDITIONS TO ACCRETIVE HOUSES	65

PART II

seven	DETAILING	75
	Chimneys; Roofs; Gables; Eaves; Dormers; Half-timbering; Tile-hanging; Brickwork; Stone; Doors; Windows; Craftmanship	

ACKNOWLEDGEMENTS	139
Index of Architects	140
Index of Places	141
List of Illustrations	142

PART I

"...Far, far below me roll the Coulsdon woodlands,
White down the valley curves the living rail,
Tall, tall, above me, olive spikes the pinewoods,
Olive against blue-black, moving in the gale.

'Deep down the drive go the cushioned rhododendrons,
Deep down, sand deep, drives the heather root,
Deep the spliced timber barked around the summer-house,
Light lies the tennis-court, plaintain underfoot.
What a winter welcome to what a Surrey homestead!
Oh! the metal lantern and white enamelled door!
Oh! the spread of orange from the gas-fire on the carpet!
Oh! the tiny patter, sandalled foorsteps on the floor!

'Fling wide the curtains! – that's a Surrey sunset
Low down the line sings the Addiscombe train,
Leaded are the windows lozenging the crimson,
Drained dark the pines in the resin-scented rain."

John Betjeman; from 'Love in a Valley', *Continual Dew* (1937)

'...though such places as Loseley and Sutton testify to Surrey's one-time wealth in great houses, it is perhaps in its smaller architecture that the county may most reasonably boast. It is unquestionably the favourite county for the homes of those whose who work in London, and this eminence in the favour of Londoners is no new thing. As far back as the reigns of Elizabeth and James I, the servants of the Court aimed to make enough - to ensure retirement to a small estate in Surrey. To them, and to the latter race of wealthy citizens of London, we owe the numerous small houses which fixed the type of local architecture. It is therefore a happy event when the designers of modern houses are found following straightly in the paths of their forerunners and building in the traditional way'.
Lawrence Weaver, *Small Country Houses of Today* (1910)

Surrey 'was so remote in the Middle Ages that it does not possess a large medieval parish church; - it has been in the forefront of English architecture only once, in 1900, and has since seen the endless debased multiplication of the type of building it pioneered. A history of English medieval architecture could be written without mentioning a single Surrey building; a history of the suburb or the folly could almost be written without going outside the county.'
Nairn and Pevsner, *Surrey* Buildings of England Series (1971)

one

THE MAKING OF THE SURREY STYLE

The habit of wealthy Londoners retiring to Surrey, which has now been going on for at least four hundred years, has meant that the county has always been swamped with money. However, because the farm land was poor, the county has rarely appealed to the plutocrat intent on building up a vast estate with a grand house. Instead, it was chosen by the comfortably wealthy - courtiers and merchants - who did not feel the need for broad acres to support their wealth, and it was this gentry class that built the small manor houses that abound in the county. Up till the middle years of the 19th century few people had much concern for the simple vernacular houses of the countryside, but from about 1860, when the railways came, all this changed. Surrey became easy to get to from London and so the county's vernacular style was one of the first to be studied with growing expertise; it was not long before the professional architect came to study Surrey buildings so that he could model his own designs on these historic precedents. This began in the early l860s - with some rather gawky architecture. But by the l870s Norman Shaw and Ralph Nevill had become interested in the Surrey style and by the end of the century numberless excellent architects were able to handle the vernacular. The style became immensely popular not only in Surrey but all over Britain and North America.

This has meant that Surrey probably now has more houses of the highest quality in the vernacular manner than any other county in Britain. However at the same time it probably has fewer authentically untouched old buildings than most counties. For the wealth of the house owners of Surrey has meant that there have always been people of means able to restore or rebuild any dilapidated cottage that came on the market, with uneven results. This of course is still going on. Nonetheless the majority of these houses were treated with knowledge if not always with a sensitivity that would be looked for (though rarely found) today.

The influx of new comfortably off Surrey residents, generated by commuter railways, meant that, from about 1870 until 1940, there was also a great deal of building of medium size houses. Here Surrey was extremely fortunate, for during this period (which more or less encompasses the Arts and Crafts Movement) some of the very best English architects built some of their finest houses in the county. These included the major figures: R. Norman Shaw, Philip Webb, C.F.A.Voysey and Ernest Newton; many lesser known yet equally able architects like Thackeray Turner, C.Harrison Townsend and M.H.Baillie Scott built important works in Surrey. Then there are a third group of architects: men little known outside the county, but whose influence was great within its borders. One such architect was Ralph Nevill of Godalming whose book *Old Cottage and Domestic Architecture in South West Surrey* we will be using a good deal. Another was, Harold Falkner, who transformed, not to say recreated, Farnham in the early years of this century.

CREATORS OF THE SURREY STYLE

It is the work of these turn of the century artists and architects, with their profound love and knowledge of the simple building styles of the neighbourhood, their appreciation of the way in which the houses lie in the Surrey landscape, and the plant life found there - the indiginous oak and pine, or such exotics as rhododendrons which have found a second home here blossoming as happily amongst the pines of Surrey as the deodars of the Himalayas - that we shall be looking to as guides to the Surrey Style. The most important were:

Edwin Lutyens Architect (1869-1944)

Gertrude Jekyll Artist Craftswoman Gardener (1843-1932)

The most important creator of the Surrey style, as we know it today, was that great master of architectural form and the Surrey vernacular, Edwin Lutyens, who, with another child of 'Old West Surrey' (as she was to name it in a memorable book) Gertrude Jekyll, brought about one of Britain's major contributions to architecture: the Edwardian 'dream house'. Houses like Munstead Wood and Orchards, both near Godalming, built in the 1890s, had a profound influence throughout the world when they were first published. Both these masterpieces came directly out of a close study of the Surrey vernacular. Gertrude Jekyll was born in 1847 and Lutyens twenty two years later in 1869. Both oddly enough were born in London, but both came to rural Surrey, Jekyll to Bramley and then Munstead, and Lutyens to Thursley, when they were very young; both were educated at home, and both were brought up amongst the then almost completely untouched Surrey countryside.

It was Gertrude Jekyll who can be said to have first brought the 'Surrey Style' to a wider public. Not Jekyll the gardener, but Jekyll the artist, craftswoman and lover of the simple old country trades and crafts. In 1873 she and her by then widowed mother moved to Munstead Heath. Like so many young Victorian ladies Gertrude Jekyll was a watercolourist, but her work was of such quality that it was admired by John Ruskin and she became a close friend of Burne Jones. And so it was that she was in at the very inception of the Arts and Crafts movement. It was only to be expected that she was soon concerning herself with the ordinary life of the countryfolk, in what was still the un-suburban surroundings of Godalming. Although failing eyesight made her give up painting, it did not diminish her creativity. In the 1880s she turned to carving and furniture making, gardening and making a collection of all the early workmen's tools that she illustrates in *Old West Surrey* (1904).

Gardener's Cottage. Munstead Wood: The British Architect 1901

So by the time she came to commission the twenty-seven year old Lutyens to design her house Munstead Wood in a woodland garden that she had already created, she knew precisely the style and type of house that she wanted, as she explained in the marvellous description of its building in *Home and Garden* (1901). Munstead Wood, unlike so many of its imitations, is a working house. Here Gertrude Jekyll had a writing room, a workshop and a constantly evolving garden, and from here she ran a large practice, designing well over three hundred gardens. She also sold plants from what today would be called a busy garden centre.

When it was completed it was immediately obvious that between them they had created in Munstead Wood the ideal Surrey house. It was to be copied again and again all over the world, often in places where the Surrey style was as alien as would be a house by Le Corbusier, say, in Godalming High Street. Gertrude Jekyll herself, with her belief in the absolute rightness of the simple arts and crafts of the countryside (which was in practical opposition to the much more sophisticated arts and crafts rationale of men like W.R.Lethaby), had a direct effect on a number of other young architects such as Herbert Baker, Robert Lorimer, Harold Falkner and even such a seemingly un-vernacular man as C.F.A.Voysey - often meeting them for the first time in the course of her professional gardening work.

Harold Falkner Architect (1876-1963)

Harold Falkner, who might well be called Lutyens' first follower, had as profound an effect on Surrey as Gertrude Jekyll or Lutyens, but his influence did not even stretch as far as the whole of 'Old West Surrey'. Nearly all Falkner's work was concentrated in just one town: Farnham. With the local businessman, and sometime mayor, Signor Borelli, he came to dominate the town from 1897, when Falkner built the Victoria Memorial Baths, until his death at eighty-seven in 1963.

A local boy, he went to the local Grammar School and School of Art; he was articled to Reginald Blomfield, but was soon in association with the firm of vaguely *art nouveau* architects Niven and Wigglesworth. In this partnership he built a great number of Surrey style houses in and around Farnham. The town of Farnham itself is his finest monument. It can almost be said (adapting the jingle about John Nash's Regent Street) that he found Farnham Victorian, and left it all Georgian. There was but one bow windowed shop front in the centre of Farnham when he began, by the time he had finished the majority of shops had a Georgian character, a 'tradition' that later generations have alas not continued.

His most impressive achievement was the replacement of Norman Shaw's wildly out of scale bank in Castle Street with a much lower and more fitting design by the office of Guy Dawber. His own most important work was to be the Town Hall: on the corner of Castle Street and Downing Street, the scale and the detailing is one of the finest examples of 'contextualism' of the inter-war period. (cf. my article: 'Farnham, England's Williamsburg' *Thirties Society Journal No. 1 1981* which gives more details of Falkner's work in Farnham).

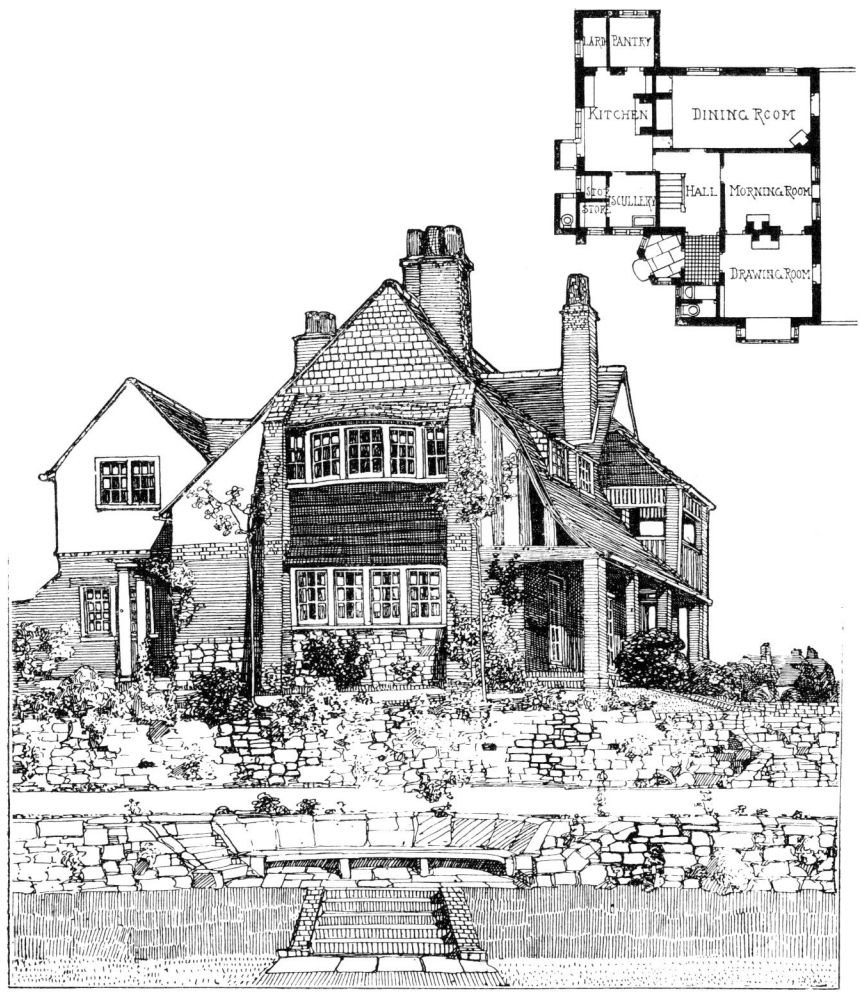

Falkner: Cottage outside Farnham: Academy Architecture 1903 ii

Charles Baily. Architect (1815-78)

Lutyens and Jekyll were by no means the first to look at the Surrey vernacular, even if, in the end, theirs was to be the strongest influence on the spread of the style throughout the world. As early as 1869, the year of Lutyens' birth, The Surrey Archaeological Society published a paper by Charles Baily: 'Remarks on Timber Houses' (republished the following year in the *Building News*). These were originally given as lectures to the Society in 1862 and 1863, during the high period of the Gothic Revival. Whilst, as one might imagine, Baily was primarily interested in elaborate old wood work, he nevertheless discusses and illustrates a number of vernacular Surrey houses, including Crowhurst Place, Great Tangley Manor, and cottages at Shere and Lingfield. At Shere he shows examples of typical Surrey chimneys and of barge-boards.

Ralph Nevill F.S.A., F.R.I.B.A. (1846-1917)

Although of different generations, Baily and Nevill knew each other through the Surrey Archaeologists; both acted as *cicerones* on the Society's regular excursions around Surrey architecture. In 1889, when Lutyens was twenty but had already started on his career, Ralph Nevill published *Old Cottage and Domestic Architecture in South-West Surrey*. This put into book form articles that had appeared in *The Builder* in 1888. Nevill, a practising architect, illustrates cottages, farms and town houses and details of their construction, with delightful drawings, many of which are held by the Surrey Archaeological Society at Guildford.

Nevill's study of the Surrey vernacular is both didactic and sensitive, and includes examples of not only large elements like chimneys, tile-hanging and cornices but also quite small details of household equipment.

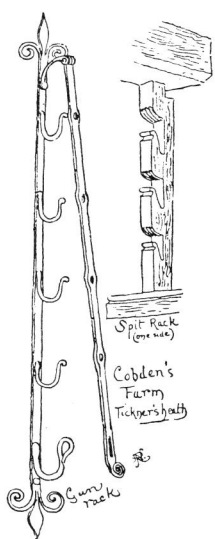

Gun and spit racks. Cobden Farm:
Ralph Nevill: Old Cottage and Domestic Architecture

Published at the very beginning of the time when every young architect was studying vernacular architecture, Nevill's drawings must have had a considerable influence on a great number of architects. One of these was

Nevill: Additions to Pinewood, Witley from The Architect 12. IX. 1870

W.Curtis Green (1875-1960), an architect and draughtsman of the highest order, who with W.Galsworthy Davie's photographs, brought out *Old Cottages and Farmhouses in Surrey (1908)*, which, with due acknowledgement, follows Nevill both in many of its examples and details. Green was writing at a time when the cottages had all largely been 'discovered' by wealthy Londoners, and so his book is inevitably less authentic than Nevill's. Both works have proved to be a goldmine of authentic detailing, and for this present book I have plundered them both quite shamelessly.

Nevill, who is hardly known at all today, is important because he is the first Surrey architect who studied the Surrey vernacular and tried to re-interpret it both in his own houses and his alterations and additions to old houses.

His was a long career: he was apprenticed to George Gilbert Scott before 1867, and his last work was, appropriately enough, the Guildford Museum in 1911. He practiced in Godalming and London and in the 1870s was responsible for a series of houses in the artistic colony that grew up around Witley. In 1875 he exhibited his additions to Pinewood, Witley at the Royal Academy. These are quite as good as the contemporary work of Norman Shaw, or G.E.Street at Holmwood (see Chapter Six) and indicate an awareness of the Surrey vernacular, in both the tile hanging and the immensely tall moulded brick chimneys, which dominate the roof and wittily combine two Surrey chimney styles. He also uses Norman Shaw-like 'aesthetic' decorations of flowers and Japanese squares in his half-timbering. In 1887 he made additions to Snowdenham Hall, Bramley for Robert Courage. The house as Nevill left it is very big, indeed it must be the largest house of its date in the Surrey cottage style. The cottages that he built on the estate, being smaller, have a much more authentic look to them. In the 1880s he made the first additions to Rake House, which he describes in *Old Cottages* as it was before his alterations. Rake is a house, which, by chance both Lutyens and Baillie-Scott were to add to in the early 20th century, (see Chapter Four).

The Artists

Like the architects, artists found Nevill's book useful. In a list of 102 subscribers published in an advertisement for the book is included such well known names as Luke Fildes, Birket Foster, Stacy Marks, Val Princeps and Marcus Stone, all of whom used old cottages as the background to their then immensely popular and rather sentimental genre paintings.

As well as these 'easel painters' there were any number of topographical artists, amateurs and professionals who painted the old buildings and villages of Surrey at that time. Many of these artists published books with titles such as *The Charm of Old Surrey*. Possibly the best of these, with illustrations by Hugh Thomson, is the *Highways and Byways* of 1908. However the artist that most captures the character of that almost lost Surrey is Helen Allingham, who lived at Witley from the 1870s until she died in 1926. She was an immensely prolific watercolourist who made her reputation with her delightful studies of old village houses. Two books which reproduced her watercolours were *The Cottage Homes of England* and *Happy England of Helen Allingham* by Marcus B. Huish; these have been recently republished. People who are about to alter their houses could do worse than to follow the details of the cottages drawn by Helen Allingham, at the same time keeping in mind Gertrude Jekyll's tougher *Old West Surrey* and *Home and Garden* as more practical reference books.

The Red Lion, Betchworth from Eric Parker: Highways and Byways in Surrey *(1909)*

*

It was very much all of a piece, it is no coincidence that Gertrude Jekyll should in 1890 have first met the very young Edwin Lutyens at the home of Harry Mangles, Littleworth Cross near Crooksbury. Mangles was one of the pioneers in the discovery and importation of rhododendrons, whose garden was then, as now, a showpiece of this new species. The house is in the Norman Shaw style by an unknown architect - indeed, could it be by Nevill?

It is sadly ironic that the products of these traditional ideas should have been taken up by continental critics who misunderstood the essentially romantic and consciously retrograde beliefs that informed the designs. Retrograde they may have seemed at the time, in so far as they were steeped in the ideals of a then rapidly passing era - but not retrograde in that it is probably here in these houses and beliefs that the seeds lie for a humane architecture of the future. It is hardly necessary to say that the belief that to be 'modern' it is essential to design in the modern style and that that style will sit readily with the architecture of any period (which it self-evidently will not) - is not followed in this book.

two

HOW & HOW NOT TO ADD TO AN OLD BUILDING

There is only one way to add to an old building of whatever period, be it medieval or 'thirties modern'. That is to study it, get to know, and if possible 'love' the building and to respect the designer of the building. Then to attempt, as far as is humanly possible, to design the additions in the manner in which you believe the original designer might himself have done. In that way, and in that way only, will additions seem to belong to the old building, so blending with the original that it gives the impression that it was always intended to look as it does now. If it is not possible to achieve this then it is probably true to say that the additions are too large and should never have been attempted.

If this route is taken it is essential to reject all doctrinaire preconceptions of style. If a building is in a clear style, be it Gothic or Classical, then clearly that style must be followed, but otherwise it would be wrong to use such a style for additions to simple country building. So we must reject that most dangerous modern heresy which under the influence of Nikolaus Pevsner, permeates so much post-war writing on architecture: that additions made in 'the style of our day and age' will grow naturally into their surroundings. Cited as an example is the way that say, a Georgian house lies naturally beside a Tudor cottage in a village street. This may be so if there is not too much discrepancy of scale or style, though there are many places where buildings of different periods do not lie happily together. This is always the case with consciously 'modern' additions. The whole basis of modern design is that it accepts machine made building components such as metal windows, large sheets of glass or even plain concrete, which are of a different scale and a different texture to the components of buildings of any earlier period. Their harsh and rectangular qualities may make them acceptable in an office block, or possibly even as a country house making a surrealist contrast all alone in a parkland setting, but machine made materials will never satisfactorily relate to old buildings. Sheet glass picture windows and flat roofed extensions, which were quite common a few years ago even in houses owned by people who believed themselves to be sensitive to old buildings, are no better than the mass produced, and mass sold, aluminium double glazing and false stone cladding of the present day; they should never be considered.

Appendix IV of Circular 8 of 1987, *Historic Buildings and Conservation Areas Policy and Procedures*, gives advice on alterations to listed buildings. Amongst such sensible suggestions as that extensions should not dominate the original building, it suggests that matching materials are not always appropriate, since *sometimes the attempted harmonious addition becomes difficult to distinguish from the original* (my italics). This is dangerous and pernicious nonsense, a development of the Pevsnerian heresy of an architecture of our own time, and should be opposed in the strongest possible manner wherever it is encountered. It all stems from the Victorian idea that each period should have an original architecture of its own time. In fact it is impossible not to build in the style of our time, even if we make every effort to design an exact replica of a past style. This can probably best be proved by considering the great Victorian Gothic Revival architects. They were considerably more learned in the Gothic than anyone is today, and on many occasions they believed that they were building exact replicas of Gothic buildings, indeed their learned contemporaries considered that they were indistinguishable from the original. To us some 150 years later these buildings seem magnificent examples of Victorian architecture, but they bear little relation to true Gothic building. However carefully we try to copy the architecture of an earlier period we will never be able to fool future generations. But if we go down this road we will at least be creating an addition that is harmonious and may well prove to be fine architecture in its own right, this we will never achieve if we approach an old building as something on which it is our duty to affix some sort of statement about the soul of architecture today. For as well as wishing to use unsympathetic materials the modern architect more often than not also wishes to make some sort of statement, making his additions as noticeably different as possible from the original. As it happens one of the earliest, and most highly praised and illustrated examples of this insensitive approach is in Surrey: Connell Ward and Lucas' The Firs at Redhill, where in 1935 they added a modern design to a bow fronted Regency house, making no effort to relate their building to the original in any way. This insensitivity was celebrated at the time and even in the *Surrey* 'Buildings of England' it is described as "a very early and very brave case of not 'keeping in keeping' ", as if that were praiseworthy. It is not and the additions to The Firs look as gauche today as they did when they were built over fifty years ago.

In any case the majority of old country buildings do not respond comfortably to too much architecture, for the vast majority of old buildings were not designed by an architect but built by a jobbing builder who, although he was a consummate craftsman (if he had not been his building

The Firs, Redhill (1935)

would be unlikely to have survived until the present time) who understood about proportions and what was fitting in his building, would none the less never consider himself to be an architect, let alone an artist. Any additions made to such a building which forces on it the personality of the author must inevitably jar. On the other hand, those few buildings which were in fact built by great designers should also never be subjected to the design whims of a modern architect/artist. They are far too precious to allow a present day architect to inflict his personality on them. Whilst this approach may not be illustrated in the fashionable architectural periodicals, the result will always be more acceptable to people using the building, or just passing by it; and that is the true functionalism and the best that any designer of any building can hope to achieve.

On the whole all additions to a building should be smaller in size than the original. Details such as windows, doors, gables and so on, must never be of a larger scale than the original nor should they be architecturally grander. If it is essential that the additions are larger than the original building then the whole original building must be recast on a grander scale whilst retaining its integrity. This needs the greatest refinement and subtlety, and should only be undertaken by someone who completely understands the style of the original building and has the wit and subtlety to create something that is both new and yet responsive to the old. This idea will be explored in the buildings discussed in Chapter Four. If only modern architects of today were to learn a simple lesson in humility and architectural subtlety then some of the disgracefully destructive work, that alas has so often been praised by the doctrinaire defenders of the modern style, would never have been built. Many of these additions are offices added to old houses, so strictly they do not come within our brief. None the less, because the county borders London, more and more of the larger houses in Surrey are being taken over as 'prestige offices', and this leads almost inevitably to large, and more often than not insensitive, additions. Since these are for commercial offices such projects are designed by large urban firms of commercial architects who have little sympathy for the Surrey countryside or for the style or scale of the old building to which they are making their additions. As well as demanding a knowledge of past styles, which few architects today are taught in the schools, it is also considerably more time consuming, and therefore expensive for the practice, to design sensitive additions to an old building. Few successful commercial architects are willing to give time to such unproductive work if they can just as easily draw from their plan chests a standard design and place it down arbitrarily whenever and wherever they are asked for a new building, whether it is suitable or not. It

E.J. May's Branksome Hilders as altered and extended for Messrs Ollivetti

is exactly this high handed attitude toward old buildings that makes architects today so universally unpopular.

Most of the old buildings illustrated in this book have been added to on numerous occasions, and many of the old buildings have been designed to give the impression that they are part of this continuing process. It is this approach, taken by all good architects, that is followed in this book, and should be followed by all people who dare to work on old buildings.

three

MAKING ADDITIONS TO OLDER BUILDINGS

Vernacular buildings of Surrey were rarely built all at one time and the Surrey style has largely come about through ordinary country builders making constant additions to these houses, not always with the same materials, but always in the same manner as the original. It was this accretive quality that so appealed to turn of the century architects who then recreated the Surrey style. For just over a decade, this style swept the world.

Over the years most old houses have undergone considerable alterations, some good and some bad. In the days before architects concerned themselves with small houses, they were added to by builders who were still working within local traditions, and it was rare that out-of-scale or out-of-keeping additions were made. Early Victorian architects were by no means as careful, a fact due largely to inexperience and lack of knowledge of vernacular details and construction. It was the generation of the 1850s and 60s, who came to see that there was something wrong with an architect inflicting his personal stylistic preferences on to old buildings, with the result that the architects of the next generation, the Arts and Crafts generation, such as Lutyens and Curtis Green, came to have a considerably more respectful approach to old buildings. They loved them and did everything that they could to preserve them and aimed to create in their own buildings houses that fitted naturally into Surrey. To understand the Surrey style we need to look at old Surrey buildings and for this we are lucky to have Nevill's clear drawings, which suggest what these cottages looked like, both in form and materials, before they were, in Curtis Green's phrase: "disfigured by the hand of the restorer."

However, it must be said that alterations were often so good that it is now almost impossible to tell what is genuinely authentic and what is the work of self-effacing late 19th century architects and builders. Nevill was sketching his Surrey houses in the 20 years before Lutyens started work. We can be certain when we are looking at Nevill's drawings that we are looking at buildings that had never been 'improved'. Of course, Nevill's drawings chronicle centuries of extensions and alterations; despite their piecemeal creation these houses work as single compositions. This fact above all others attracted the Arts and Crafts generation. Nevill is usually such a good draughtsman that we can readily work out the building history of these houses with suprising accuracy. Because of this, they can give us all the clues that we need to judge the proper fashion in which to make additions to a vernacular building.

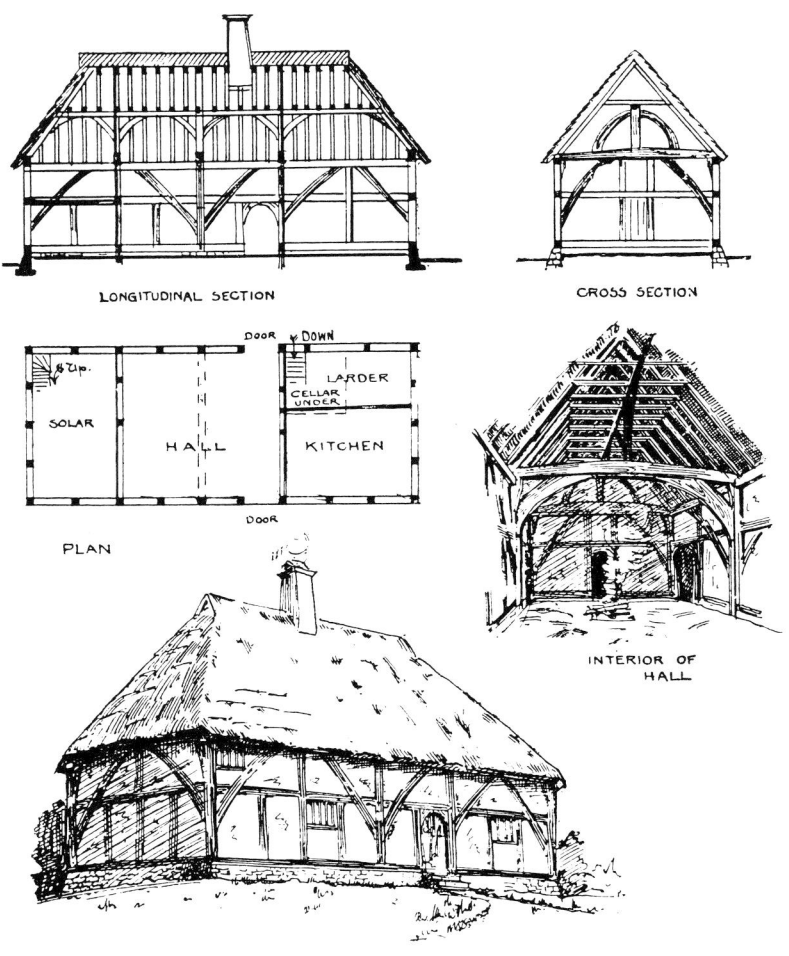

Moses Hill Farm; from Swanton and Woods Bygone Haslemere (1914)

Moses Hill Farm. This is a typical hall house, of straightforward timber framing, with a wattle and daub in-filling between the timbers. This is not completely unsophisticated, since the hall is already divided into a Solar, or private room, at one end, and at the other there is a kitchen and larder with a cellar under. There is a chimney in the centre of the roof, but as yet no fireplace; the smoke finds its own way out through a hole in the roof.

This position for the chimney was not entirely satisfactory, both because of the unpleasantness of the smoke, and more importantly, because of the danger of fire. It was not long before improvements were made and a new fireplace and chimney built in brick, in a structurally more logical position on an outside wall, became the normal practice. This would have been the first thoroughly fireproof part of the house. However the chimney on the ridge was very often retained, and a chimney in this position on an old house suggests that a hall house may be lurking somewhere within.

Summersbury Farm House in 1873. (Drawing by L.A.Shuffrey in the Architectural Association Sketch Book of 1873-4); illustrated in Curtis Green: Old Cottages and Farmhouses of Surrey (1908)

The plan shows a development from the simple hall plan of Moses Hill Farm. To the west the Solar has been extended to become a parlour, though that of course is a relatively modern name, with a large deep fireplace, which supports no less than three chimney stacks, two presumably serving the upstairs rooms, which are approached from a new staircase which has been added beside the chimney.

On the east side of the hall, there have been further additions to the service areas. The kitchen has been much extended south, first with a gabled extension. If Shuffrey's plan is to be believed, this must be supported by a beam within the roof since it has in its turn been added to with an extension for the oven which has its own small chimney.

To the north there is another extension, with a dairy, Shuffrey illustrates a lead ventilator window here. Nevill has a similar (but not identical) detail, which he says comes from a house near Godalming, but knows of no others extant in 1888; *Old West Surrey* illustrates a very much simpler design. The great advantage of these ventilators is that they follow the shape of whatever leaded windows are used, they are decorative and they do not affect the overall shape of the window, as an opening ventilator inevitably must. Since it is still possible to cast lead or for that matter aluminium, which would here make a perfectly suitable substitute, there seems to be little reason why these cannot be used in leaded windows today.

THE SURREY STYLE

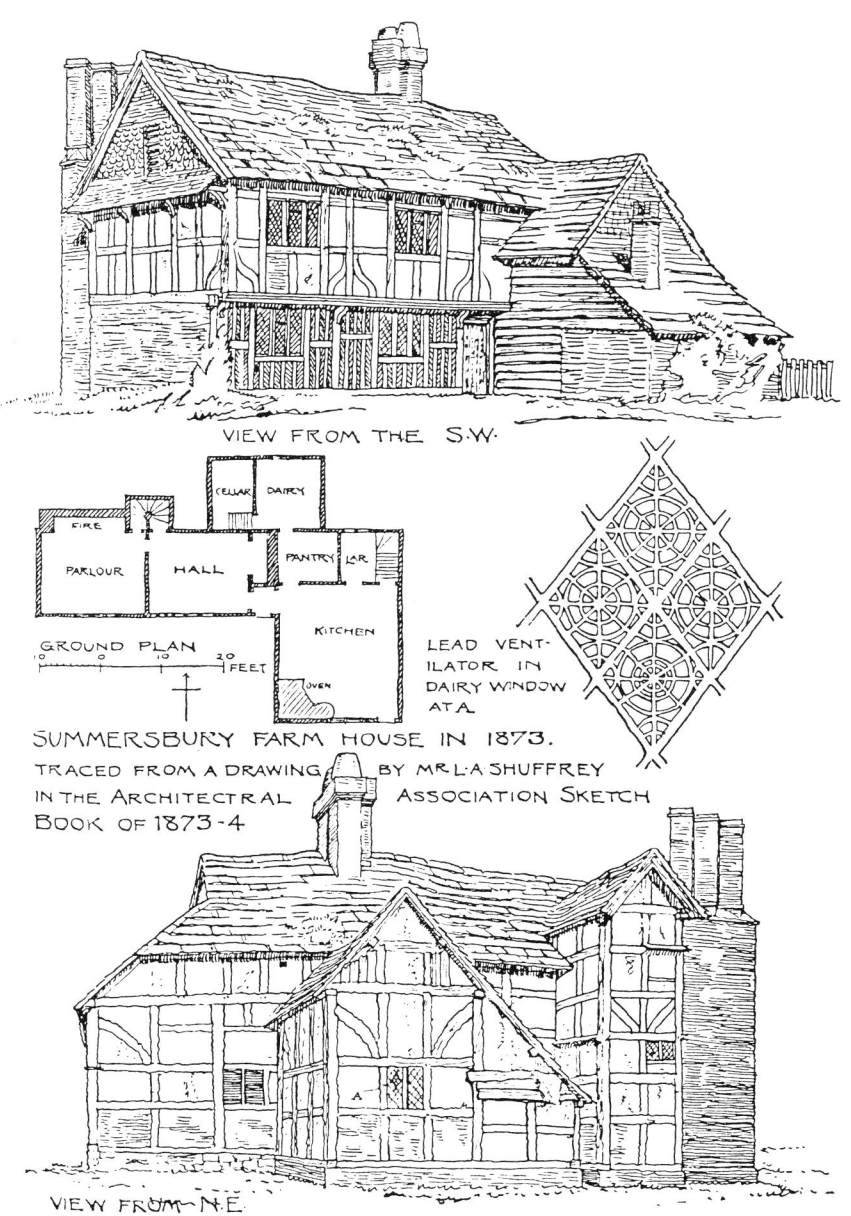

The additions to the plan become obvious when we look at the accretive elevations, which here seem to have come about naturally, though none the less the result in its seemingly haphazard balance is entirely pleasing.

The south west elevation, being the entrance elevation, is the more elaborate, and also retains more of the old hall visible. The building is almost entirely half-timbered, the upper part being slightly jettied out over the lower. The windows are presumably later made additions when the hall was divided to make an upper floor. On the left the gable is tile-hung with a characteristic kick at the bottom, to stop the rain water from running down the wall and rotting the timbers.

The way in which the relatively late clapboarded kitchen addition has been handled should he noted. The lower gable end runs flush with the half hip of the roof which can be seen on the north east elevation. A cat-slide roof in its turn develops out of the gable. Whilst this addition is clearly later, and built in cheaper materials, it none the less seems to belong to the older building, because it seems to have grown naturally from the earlier form. It is important that whenever additions are made great care be taken in achieving this seemingly natural growth.

On the north east elevation the additions dominate the old building, though they none the less keep well within the natural envelope of the form. On the left is the dairy extension, with a roof coming down very low over the cellar entrance. To the right is the tall staircase block. Beyond this again is the fine brick block of the new chimneys, which, whether intentionally or not, are placed in such a position that they make a perfect stop to the facade. Note how, other than the chimneys, all the extensions are half- timbered to match the existing building. All the half- timbering is built on a brick sleeper wall, so that rain and damp on the ground cannot rot the timbers.

Nursecombe Bramley. This hall plan house has been added to in a more elaborate manner. Whilst the main roof runs through, it has been almost swamped with two short gabled wings, and then beyond the entrance porch an extension has been covered with a roof that continues down sweeping almost to the ground. This is as effective a method of terminating a facade as was the solid block of a tall chimney at Summersbury.

The placing and the slightly different size of the three gables, each with different decorative barge boards, is extremely effective. Notice that the left hand gable is slightly smaller, with the result that the ridge joins just below the main ridge of the house, thus allowing a small gablet to make a clear indication of the end of the roof ridge. These gablets were originally open and devised to let out the smoke from the halls before the advent of chimneys; however they are such a common feature of Surrey houses of all periods, that it would seem that the form was retained well after it had any practical function. The central gable wing is wider and so its ridge breaks just above the main ridge. The small gable to the porch is considerably lower, and jettied over the front door; this jettying seems to be at the same height as the eaves of the lowered roof, which would make sense from the point of view of construction.

Nursecombe Bramley, Nevill: Old Cottages and Domestic Architecture in S.W. Surrey

Nursecombe also seems to have been half-timbered, with tile-hung gables. By the 1880s this had been at some time plastered over, probably in an attempt to counteract damp, though it is quite possible that the timbers were never intended to be shown, which was true of the vast majority of less pretentious buildings.

Gomshall. Here again two gabled wings are added to the main hall house, and again the ridge of the left hand gable comes just a little lower than the ridge of the main roof, but otherwise there is little similarity with Nursecombe. This house is architecturally very much more pretentious. In the end gable the half-timbering is very elaborate, a display piece always intended to be seen. The end of the house is supported by great chunky chimneys built over a wide fireplace; because the chimney stack was tacked on to a half- timbered building, there was a freedom to give it expression.

On the right the gable is considerably thinner so that the main roof dominates it both at its ridge and eaves. However it projects well forward of the left hand gable so an architectural balance is struck. Notice also the way in which the main roof at this end is run up above the ridge to the large chimney, which is built a short distance off the ridge. This has an entirely practical purpose since this treatment means that any leaves or rainwater will not gather in a place that is always vulnerable to leaks: the flashing area where the chimney comes through the roof. It is remarkable how often what seems at first glance a picturesque conceit turns out to be an entirely practical detail, brought about more often than not by the necessity in this country to counteract rain penetration.

Gomshall Nevill: Old Cottages

Cranleigh. This cottage is of humbler stock than Gomshall with a single wing addition. The ridge of the addition is much lower than the main ridge, the eaves are allowed to run through level, the wing to the side by the front of the house is half timbered, whereas that to the front is tile-hung with the lower courses skirted out to form a cover to the two back doors. The treatment of the gable end is highly eccentric. It starts with a gablet, then a half hip which develops into a tile-hung gable, which, in its turn, changes pitch lower down.

At Cranleigh, Nevill: Old Cottages

On the other side a single storey addition has been made, with the single pitch roof built up against the gable. However the top of this roof pitches above the height of the eaves. Normally this would have meant bringing the main roof out to form a small hip here, but this would result in a weak junction; the solution arrived at here, with a very small gable rising above the eaves, is much more elegant.

Dunsfold Common. Nevill: Old Cottages

The *Dunsfold Common* cottage is of much the same form as at Cranleigh. Once again on the left there is a lean-to roof, and to the right a wing projects with a gable that runs down low on the right, but here everything is much calmer, and the effects are achieved without the agitation of Cranleigh. However, the fact that the cottage is completely tile-hung above the head of the ground floor windows makes for a certain blandness. The way in which the lean-to roof to the left comes in at exactly the point of the eaves means that the builder has not needed to go to the elaboration, or cost, of the Cranleigh detail.

Jerrys, Pirbright 1906. A remarkable example of a simple extension covered by a single sweeping roof, creating the type of 'pure form' so admired by architects such as Curtis Green.

Jerrys, Pirbright; Photographic Survey of Surrey, Surrey Local Studies Library, Guildford

Compton. (Plate i; opposite) A variation of a typical Surrey type, much admired and copied by the Surrey architects of the Arts and Crafts period, this time seen from the rear. Notice here the way in which the lean-to roof is carried right up into the main roof to form a hip, none the less the builder has still had to make recourse to the Cranleigh solution of a small gable at the eaves.

Although this is quite a small building it should not be thought of as an unsophisticated cottage. This is no agricultural worker's hovel, but the small house of a well to do yeoman or farmer. This can be seen in the two major elements, the great horizontal sweep of the roof offset by the immensely large and tall chimneys. It can never have been functionally necessary to build such large chimneys, but like Lutyens in a later period, the builders of these houses saw the aesthetic need to counter the strong horizontals of their roofs with a strong upwards thrust of the powerful chimneys.

Plate i

Compton; Nevill: Old Cottages and Domestic Architecture

Plate ii

Gertrude Jekyll: Autochrome of Munstead Wood. Country Life

Plate iii

Helen Allingham: The Fish Shop, Haslemere. *Reproduced by permission of Marley plc*

Plate iv

Field Place, Dunsfold. Nevill: Old Cottages

ADDITIONS TO OLDER BUILDINGS

Field Place, Dunsfold. (opposite. Pl. iv) This rear view of a farm house is probably the most complicated of Nevill's examples and shows the way in which complex additions may he made whilst still retaining the integrity of the building. The main hall can just be made out, with its tall chimney in the centre of the block, a big dormer breaking the roof-line just below it. Onto this has been added a quite seperate block, with its own chimney breast; attached to it are a series of low outbuildings, each with their own roof. The whole elaborate building has retained its integrity because all the additions are built of the same materials, presumably Bargate stone with tile roofs, and in Nevill's picture the eaves line on the main block runs round level so the later wings do not dominate the older building. Like so many of these examples there is a natural balance of form; the two large chimneys reflect each other and have precisely the right amount of weight to set off the complex horizontals of the roofs.

Although it would be a brave designer who attempted to copy such complexity, there is little reason why all additions should blandly attempt to exactly follow the original building, certainly on a number of occasions Lutyens created highly complex forms in his additions, as did W.D.Caroe at Vann, (see Chapter Four).

Coster's Farm in 1890; Surrey Local Studies Library, Guildford

THE SURREY STYLE

Coster's Farm, Ockley. (previous page) The gabled wing does not project very far forward of the hall, nevertheless, when a further small extension was needed, the roof of the gable was continued down. An interesting example of the way a minor extension can be made into a telling part of the character of a building.

Old Cottages, Betchworth; Surrey Local Studies Library, Guildford.

ADDITIONS TO OLDER BUILDINGS

View from the keep, Farnham Castle, looking towards castle street and The Borough. 1905 Surrey Local Studies Library, Guildford.

Cottages at Betchworth in 1890. (on page 34). The additions to the cottage are fascinating, particularly the large dormer, whose ridge is at the same level as the main roof ridge. Normally nowadays it is assumed that a window in a dormer must take up the full expanse of the front face. Here an entire room has been built out from the roof as a dormer, whilst the window that lights it is quite small. This is a very difficult detail to bring off, since it is very easy to make the dormer too dominant, but here it just about succeeds because of.the great size of the otherwise unbroken sweep of roof. The small wing with its gable and chimney do not affect this, though they certainly add interest to what would otherwise be a rather bland building.

View from the keep, Farnham Castle. (previous page). A rare photograph, if only because it shows, from an unusual view, Castle Street Farnham before Harold Falkner and Signor Borelli made their alterations. Norman Shaw's out-of-scale bank building can just be made out rearing up at the end of the street on the left.

This is printed here, however, because of the additions to the back of the houses in Castle Street. From the front these houses suggest the almost uniform unbroken line of a Georgian street, yet from the back it is clear that they are far from uniform and date from a number of periods. To the backs are added a series of out-houses, most of them with hipped roofs but all of them different, thus showing some of the many variations that are available to a designer when extending a building with a pitched roof. The house at the top of the hill to the left has a simple hipped roof addition, then there is much more elaborate addition. A weather-boarded privy seems to have been added at first floor level, and beyond this there is a pair of hipped roofs with gablets (which here surely can never have been designed to let out smoke) joined together, a form that Lutyens much enjoyed. Beyond this again there is a gabled extension which has in its turn been extended with a low hipped roof over bay windows.

four

ADDITIONS BY ARCHITECTS WORKING IN THE VERNACULAR TRADITION

The three houses looked at in this chapter are large by today's standards, but such is the nature of the architectural vocabulary of the Surrey vernacular, its details and motifs can be employed on all sizes of building, the eventual composition being the vital factor.

GREAT TANGLEY MANOR

Great Tangley Manor is one of the finest of the small Surrey houses, (*Surrey* Buildings of England calls it "the most impressive of Surrey's moderate collection of half-timbered houses") so it is well documented. It is also of considerable interest since that great Arts and Crafts architect, Philip Webb, worked here for about twenty years from the late 1880s. Nairn in the Buildings of England, calls this work "one of the first nineteenth century additions to an existing house to attempt to reproduce the spirit and deliberately avoid reproducing the letter of the old work." This puts into a nutshell precisely what it was that the architects of that period were striving to attain, and there could be no better guide than Philip Webb, to anyone proposing to add to an old house.

Although the very elaborate half-timber work to the entrance front is dated 1584, this is in fact a fronting of a much older, and very fine hall house, with a splendid and rather elaborate roof truss, which was lost to view when the hall was divided horizontally to give first floor bedrooms. This detail was drawn and published as early as 1869 by Charles Baily. Of course, Philip Webb, good SPAB anti-scrape man that he was, carefully left this floor in when he made his restorations.

When Baily recorded the house in the early 1860s, it had obviously been divided up, a garden wall separates two parts of the house. From the look of the chimneys the manor was in a bad way. Indeed, in 1889 Nevill says that: "Tangley was, some years ago, in a very poor state, but it has happily fallen into kindly hands which have zealously preserved the old work". This was Wickham Flower, who bought the house in 1884 and for the next eighteen years, until his death, worked on the careful repair of the house with Philip Webb.

As Gertrude Jekyll says: "This eminent architect set his face entirely

The main frontage; from 'Remarks on Timber Houses' by Charles Baily Surrey Archaeological Collections IV 1869.

The roof above the hall.

against any renewal that should be in direct imitation of the old work; and when, later, another sitting-room and more bedrooms were required, and he built a library at the eastern end, it was done in such a way that it assumed no effect of competition with the timbered front. It is perfectly in harmony, but gives the impression of voluntarily effacing itself in order to enhance the older work" (*Country Life*, 21.1.1905)

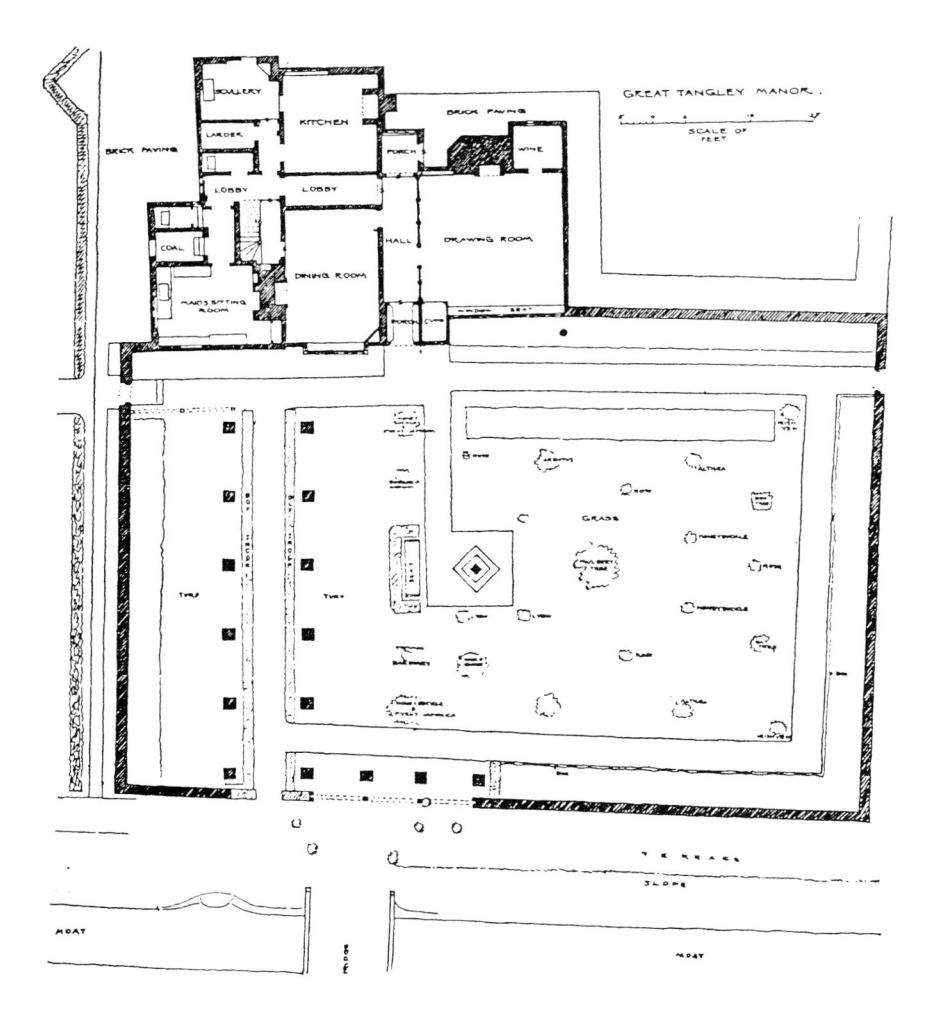

Curtis Green: Plan after Philip Webb; Cottages and Farmhouses in Surrey

THE SURREY STYLE

Nevill: Old Cottages *(Top Facing). Bedford Lemere; dated 1889; (Bottom Facing). R.C.H.M.E. Tangley in 1904, (Above).* Country Life

The photograph, taken in 1889, shows Webb's simple addition of a small hipped roof wing which, from the plan, seems to contain staff rooms. Note the chimney which makes no effort to copy the existing chimneys, but is a typical Webb chimney, which runs up very straight and broad to a small tile capped roof. This is a favourite motif of a number of architects, such as Edwin Lutyens and E.J.May, who considered themselves followers of Webb. In the garden, Webb built an elaborate, roofed timber bridge over the moat, and a series of tile capped Bargate stone walls, linked with oak pergolas, which were to have a profound effect on Edwin Lutyens when he came to work with Gertrude Jekyll on his architectural gardens.

This is not the end of the story. After Wickham Flower died the house was sold and in 1902 George Jack, Webb's assistant since 1880, made further additions to the house. These Jekyll felt to be too overpowering. *Country Life* again: "Mr Webb was of opinion (sic) that nothing more could possibly be added without serious loss to the character of the building, a conviction that would seem to appear justified by the effect of some recent additions at the eastern end. It provides a large and handsome music-room and some bedrooms, all on the ground floor and makes Great Tangley a larger and more commodious country house. The work is excellent and, considering the size of the additions, it is, perhaps, as little obtrusive as possible. But there can be no doubt that it overloads the old house, and takes much of its charm." Webb was of course right, all buildings have their natural size, and it is well nigh impossible to make sensitive additions larger than that natural size.

Since 1905 Great Tangley has alas been further added to, altered and then, as must inevitably happen when a house becomes over-large, it has been split up. And so we return to the 1860s, with a divided house. But this time although the house is now in very good condition, there is little chance that it will ever be a single home again.

Great Tangley, back view, after 1945; Surrey County Council.

RAKE HOUSE, MILFORD

Much the same tale is to be told of Rake House. The original house was built in 1602, the date is carved on one of the mantelpieces. Nevill drew a plan and recorded the two frontages as they were before 1882. It is an early example of the move away from the hall house. Nevill was convinced that the 'hall' here was always the kitchen, whilst the two private living rooms ran in a wing at right angles to this, a very sophisticated idea in an ordinary house in the country of this period. But then Rake was built by Henry Bell who was Clerk Comptroller to the household of James I.

The staircase is also interesting. This is said to be an early example of the development of the newel staircase. At Rake the stairs are built square around four posts, which run from floor to ceiling. Before that, stairs had been built in a turret with all the steps angled from a circular column, (as can be seen at Summersbury, page 26). Later the tall posts used at Rake were reduced to become newel posts.

Rake was also of great character on the outside. It is very largely half-timbered with a fine display of rather complex forms on the east front. Here a long wing ran north whilst a half-timbered gabled cross wing, which contained the south facing parlour, makes a stop on the south. In the corner formed there is another gabled block which holds the staircase. On the other side overlooking a lake there are two tile-hung gables between a vast chimney, made of one flue placed diagonally between two square blocks (see page 79). Below there is a single storey hipped lean-to which Nevill believed to have been added later; whether this is so or not the whole makes an interesting and cohesive elevation.

In the early 1880s, Nevill was called in to repair Rake, and make additions. His fine tall red brick moulded chimney, like the chimneys at Pinewood, that runs across the roof ridge, has style. His extension follows Webb's credo of building in the same style but with no direct copying: mark that the half-timbering on the new entrance front gable is unlike the old work, though materials, scale and the line of the eaves are, of course, adhered to. Considering the size of the new work, Nevill has been inventive. The sole unsuccessful feature is the small gable on the garden front where a chimney runs up with two windows close on either side. This trick seems to have been an idiosyncracy of the man. Lawrence Weaver is hardly fair when he says of these that he "carried out his restorations at a time when such work was so not well understood - and the building suffered somewhat." (*Small Country Houses: their repair and enlargement 1914.*)

Nevill: Entrance front before 1882; Old Cottages

Nevill: Proposed alterations; The Architect July 9th 1881

ADDITIONS BY ARCHITECTS

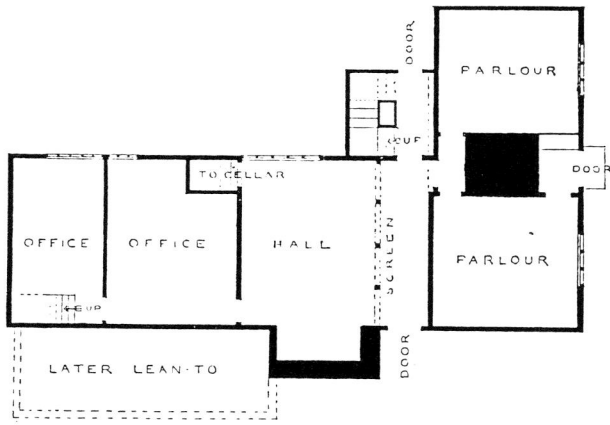

Nevill; Plan, 1882; Old Cottages

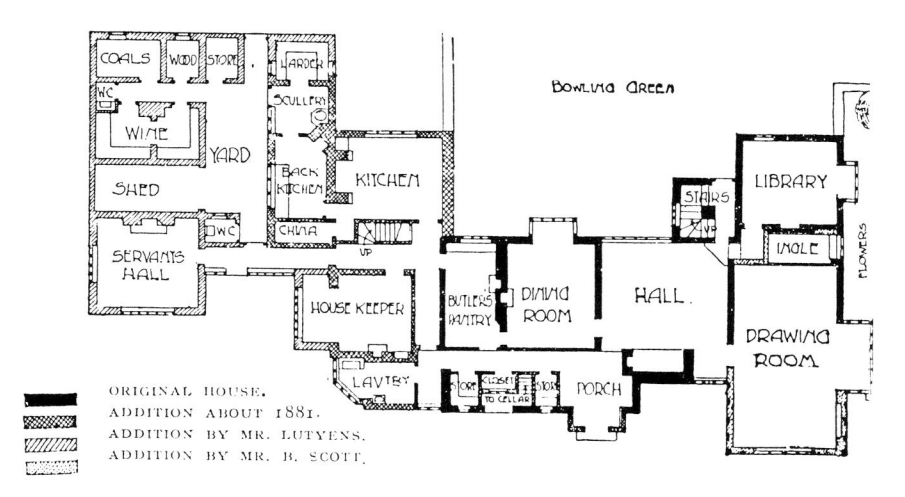

Plan showing extensions and alterations The Studio, 1908

    Nevill's work preserved Rake and left it a manageable size, which cannot be said of the house after it had been gone over by two much more distinguished architects. In 1897, Lutyens, in the first flush of his early success, was commissioned by a new owner to add a new service wing. This was one of the problems of Edwardian architecture, as Jill Franklin has shown in *The Gentleman's Country House and its plan* 1853-1914 (1981). Servicing the needs of even such a modest house as Rake required a great

THE SURREY STYLE

Nevill: Rake before 1882; Old Cottages

Nevill: Proposed Additions; The Architect July 9th 1881

Rake Manor in 1908; Country Life

many staff. Lutyens added a Butler's Pantry, House-keeper's room, two kitchens, a scullery and a larder, two stores for wine and wood and a coal store, a yard, a shed and two WCs.

These late Victorian service wings are a serious problem for anyone concerned with old buildings. Although today even the greatest of mansions does not require this amount of service areas, it is often very difficult to remove them. When, as here at Rake, the additions are made by a very fine architect, whose work sometimes may be more notable than the original building, the only solution seems to be to keep the service wing and divide it off, making it into a separate house. Which in fact is what has happened at Rake.

The departure of Lutyens was not the end of the story. In 1907, the house having changed hands again, the new owner commissioned M.H.Baillie Scott to make further additions. As it happens Lutyens had not been asked to much alter the original body of the house; this Baillie Scott now did. He very considerably lengthened the southern wing, bringing it forward to the pond and forming a grand drawing room. On the south here he built a large two storey bay with leaded lights in oak mullions, giving it a hipped roof, very much in the Lutyens manner. He also built a separate half-timbered entrance lodge.

The result of all this work is that Rake had now become a very large house, in fact too large a house for today's living, and so it has had to be divided.

Nowadays of course it is rarely necessary to add vast service wings to houses, but old houses are still being added to, usually because a new and alien use is found, which can often lead to disastrous results. Sometimes this is done because a company wishes to acquire 'prestige offices', but more often the building becomes a school with all that that means in new and tinny ancillary buildings. Schools go bankrupt and when these extended houses come on the market again they more often than not are no longer of interest to the ordinary house buyer however wealthy he may be, which means that they are forever sterilized into institutional use. However there have been some recent cheering cases where schools have been made back at great expense, and with a great deal of demolition, into private houses again.

VANN

The story of Vann is different from that of Rake, though it also is of an old house extended by an Edwardian architect. For Vann was made into a family house for his own family by the Arts and Crafts church architect W.D.Caroë. In 1908 he obviously judged his family's requirements right since it is still lived in by his grandson, Martin, and his family. Martin Caroë still carries on the practice, from London and Vann, just as his father and grandfather did before him.

Plate v

Vann, new wing and pergola to right. Photographed by André Goulancourt

Plate vi

Corridor link to barn

Plate vii

The Forecourt

Plate viii

The Music Room in the barn

ADDITIONS BY ARCHITECTS

The main block of Vann was a farmhouse built at the end of the 16th century, with beside it on the road a great 17th century barn. It was lived in by the Jennings family and sold in 1490 by Thomas Jennings, who was to be great grandfather to Sarah Jennings, Duchess of Marlborough. In 1689 it was bought by the Mayor of Guildford who added a small brick drawing room in the Dutch manner.

That was much as it was when Mr and Mrs Caroë found the house in 1908, and they took it immediately. House and barn were in a deplorable condition, as were so many rural buildings at that time. Followers of William Morris and the Society for the Protection of Ancient Buildings, they set about their work of repair and extensions with the greatest care. The main rooms of the old house were stripped of a whole series of staircases and partitions, to bring it back to its original condition; Vann, like so many Surrey manors, had been divided into a number of cottages.

The old house which ran North and South was made into the main family core, whilst a new entrance, kitchens and a service wing were formed into an entrance courtyard on the north. Mrs Caroë used to put on concerts, masques and theatrical shows, and the barn seemed perfect for this. Caroë converted a line of pig-sties into a wide book-lined passage which became an open area, linking the barn with the old building to the south and the new service wing to the north, thus creating the type of flowing space that was beginning to become popular in houses where the artistic people gathered. Lutyens used wide passages; Baillie Scott liked great halls from which most of the other rooms grew; on the other side of the Atlantic, Frank Lloyd Wright and the brothers Greene, influenced there by the Japanese, joined their living rooms in one continual flow of space. What makes it so interesting here is that Vann is one of the few examples where this spatial flow is used in an old house, for old houses with their small rooms do not usually lend themselves to this treatment. It was clever of Caroë to realise that he could achieve this by making his open corridor a link between the various diffuse elements of the interior.

Caroë was also very careful to see to it that these elements melded together on the outside of the house so that, whilst his details do not attempt to copy anything on the original house it is practically impossible to tell what is old and what is W.D.Caroë, so carefully does he see to it that his new building materials and the workmanship of the builders match in with the old. He went to great length to achieve this. For instance the barn had to be reclad with new materials, both because the old timber was rotten but also to insulate it. Asbestos boards being considered at that time best for this purpose, Caroë, a most practical architect, mellowed the rawness of the new timber facing by floating the boards on the pond for the winter. Those boards being considered at that time best for this purpose, Caroe, a most practical architect, mellowed the rawness of the new timber facing by floating the boards on the pond for the winter. Those boards that were not water-logged at the end came out a wonderful old silver colour. They were then fixed to the asbestos cladding with brass screws, which were concealed behind zinc studs. All the new roof tiles were dipped in blood from the butcher's to reduce their brash newness.

Everything was done to make the house as comfortable and modern as possible, whilst retaining its original character. All the floors were taken up, and a waterproof concrete flooring was laid, then the boards were put back, just as they had been before. The house was lit by electricity almost from the beginning and there were garages as well as stables built around the entrance court.

This made an only slightly formal entrance with the porch to the house on the centre of the south side. On the other side of the house it is a little more formal, with a long pergola running out eastwards to a water garden at a small lake. Between the two wings to the southwest there is a formal rose garden, whilst south of the pergola is a wilder garden. These gardens, in which Gertrude Jekyll had a hand, are designed to compliment the house, to give outdoor living spaces so that the house and the garden are interlocked. All has been looked after so well by three generations of the Caroes, that today the whole complex seems to be one, and seems at no time to have been consciously designed, but to have grown naturally.

This was the ideal that Caroë and his contemporaries were working towards when they took in hand an old house, realising that it was their job not just to pass on a repaired old building to future generations, but at the same time to retain the essential character of an old building. This is something that is rarely attempted today in our often distressingly coarse work, (time and love being more lacking than money), but it is as legitimate to aim for this at the end of the 20th Century as it was at its beginning.

five

THE NEW SURREY STYLE

To the generation of architects of the late 19th century, the simple Surrey vernacular style had great attractions. They were reacting against the harsher tenets of the Gothic revival, but not altogether rejecting its ideals. Specifically they still believed that it was better to follow the traditional native forms of building rather than accept the unsuitable continental imports.

Philip Webb was the architect most celebrated, among architects, to uphold the native traditions of building. To the general public he was little known, seldom publishing his works in periodicals. His fellow apprentice from the office of George Edmund Street was the very different Richard Norman Shaw. Shaw was admired for his flamboyant perspectives which succeeded in implying that his new houses had been added to by successive generations of yeomen. Shaw built a great deal in Surrey in his half timbered, tile-hung, semi-vernacular style. All the same, his "Old English" look is perhaps too national to capture the specifically Surrey traditions of building. His houses are too large and too pretetious for what is essentially a style derived from cottages and the houses of artisans. It it perhaps a telling fact that none of Shaw's country houses in Surrey have remained undivided private houses, whereas most of Lutyens' grand commissions remain happily as family homes.

Nevill's work was a local part of the Norman Shaw "Old English" style and a part of the renewed interest in traditional styles of building. He takes us back to the basics of composition and construction. *The Architect's* review of his book, saw "in the cottages and farmhouses represented ... efforts to overcome difficulties .. not unlike those which beset most of us in practice." In Nevill we can see where the Surrey style began, in this chapter we will look at how it developed in the hands of Surrey architects, like Thackeray Turner and Edwin Lutyens into a 'new' Surrey style.

House at Shere. Most of Nevill's examples are of relatively small farmers' houses which have over the years had various additions though the main form of the original hall house remains visible. At Shere, however,

Nevill shows a more complex house. Although he illustrates it he has nothing to say about it except to comment on the chimney. The house, with its haphazard balance, its contrasting chimneys and its simple detailing, encapsulates exactly what it was that the vernacular revival architects were aiming at when they built from scratch. The photograph of 1908 might be the picture of a contemporary house.

Galsworthy Davie: At Shere; Curtis Green: Farmhouses and Cottages

    On the left of the picture there is a great chimney breast, which contains an ingle, above sail detached star chimneys of unusual size (as Nevill says). To the left of this a wing runs off in which there are two dormer windows, the dormers formed by a change in slope of the roof; below is the porch to the back door.
    On the front elevation the first part of the wall is quite tall with leaded windows at the first and ground floors. In Nevill's drawing, the block appears to be stopped by a single thick stumpy chimney which runs up the wall plane - a favourite late Victorian trick; (Galsworthy Davie's photograph shows that the chimney is in fact on the ridge and that Nevill's drawing is capable of two readings). Beyond, at the centre of the frontage, roof eaves come down much lower and the roof runs along horizontally until it is stopped by a gable corbelled out over the road. It is an elevation of which

anyone from C.F.A.Voysey to Edwin Lutyens would have been proud, and it clearly indicates that there were plenty of precedents in Surrey for architects to copy when they came to design their houses.

Nevill: House at Shere; Old Cottages

Holmwood, Holmbury St. Mary 1873-6

    Shaw's master, the great Gothic Revivalist George Edmund Street, also turned to the "Old English" style at the end of his life when, between 1873 and 1876, he built for himself in Surrey the wonderfully accretive house of Holmwood at Holmbury St Mary. Holmwood is not entirely in the Surrey vernacular manner, indeed it suggests that perhaps part of it was the hall of a medieval abbey. Built of stone with two tall tracery windows and a Gothic stone porch, at one end there is clearly a solar which has a half-timbered gabled roof with decorative barge boarding. At the back there is a stone look-out tower. To one side of this, there has been added, (we are clearly meant to believe) at a later date, a secondary domestic wing. At ground level there is stone, the first floor above is half timbered with brick infill and

Holmwood, Holmbury, St. Mary; The Architect June 6th 1874

the four gables over are tile hung. To one side there is a more temporary seeming half-timbered addition attached to a light covered way. (The house as built was modified from this perspective since the library and drawing room - the stone block on the right - were turned bodily and ran on from the porch and behind the tower, instead of at the side as in this 1874 drawing.)

Above the whole building sail five groups of tall red brick Surrey chimneys, each group different from its neighbour. Very similar chimneys will be found in Nevill or Curtis Green's books.

Although the work of one of the great Gothic revivalists, Holmwood prefigures much of what architects of the next generation were successfully to accomplish. This is seen in the way in which the domestic block joins the hall, in what appears at first an haphazard manner. It is of course carefully calculated, as can be seen from the way in which the eave lines of the two wings run through at the same level, but, since they are disguised by the multitude of gables, the eaves are never clearly seen.

The way in which Street handles his chimneys is particularly interesting. These are placed with great care to balance the composition, whilst suggesting that their random position is entirely functional. Their height also is exactly calculated to create a harmonious relationship with the horizontality of the roof.

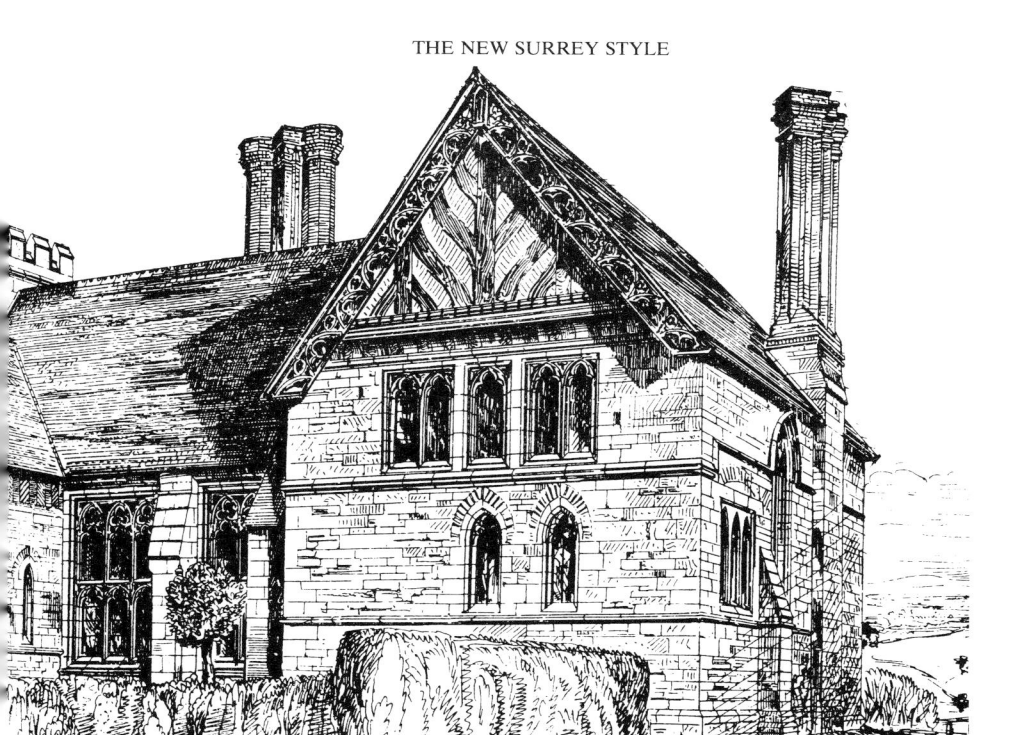

The great Gothic Revivalists originally learnt the craft of harmonious balance for their churches from a study of the Romantic water colourists of the early years of the 19th century. It is not chance that all the great vernacular revival architects learnt their craft from Gothic Revival church architects (like G.E.Street or G.G.Scott) - or their pupils (Shaw or Ernest George). An appreciation of the art of romantic composition, with its unified and harmonious balance of many disparate elements, is the key to understanding of the vernacular revival architects, and the key to the understanding of how additions to such buildings should be approached.

Westbrook, Godalming 1899-1900

Like Vann, Westbrook is an art and crafts architect's house, but unlike Vann it was a new house on a virgin site. With his partner Eustace Balfour (brother of the prime minister) Thackeray Turner built number houses and blocks of flats on the Grosvenor estate in London. He was the secretary of the Society for the Protection of Ancient Buildings from 1885 until 1911, a friend of William Morris and Philip Webb. Inevitably, when he came to build his own house, on a high hill above Godalming, he followed the strictest Arts and Crafts principles. Everything is built by hand. He used local stone for the walls, great blocks of Bargate stone quarried from the garden, local red tiles on the roof. No doubt because the stone came so readily to hand Turner felt that he could use more of it than was customary in Surrey. So the mullions to the windows are stone, (brick or oak would have been more common), as are the gables, where one might expect to find half-timbering or tile hanging, and even the chimneys are solid rectangles of stone, rather than the elaborate brickwork that we have come to expect.

Like Street's house, it is designed to look as though it has been built through generations, and in that way it sits as if it always belonged to its hill top. As Lawrence Weaver said (*Country Life* 20th Jan. 1912) Westbrook is "simple, unaffected, owing nothing, or at least singularly little, to the spirit of the Renaissance; it shows what can be done by using local materials in a straightforward yet thoughtful fashion".

Unaffected certainly, but unsophisticated it is not. The entrance court appears straightforward: the projecting wing to the left holds the kitchens, and on the right there is a high wall, in which there is a gate by which you can enter the garden through a loggia. At the centre there is a fine solid stone gabled porch with a great timber beam supported on four chunky columns. To the left, on the first floor, is a small rendered gable; this very minor addition to the facade is a perfect example of the Arts and Crafts architect's artful use of a standard old Surrey idiom. The jettied projection forms a porch to the back door; the gable breaks through the eaves-line of the main block allowing Turner to drop the eaves after turning the corner into the lesser kitchen block by suggesting a long building history. We will see Lutyens playing a similar trick at Fulbrook.

Turner has put all his living rooms on the south, and has designed them to the size and shape that he wants, without it would seem, giving much consideration as to what the result will be from the outside. The drawing room pushes right forward of the main front of the house, whilst on the other side the kitchen block, with the staff sitting room which overlooks the garden, a rarity at that time, is set well back. On the first floor the main bedroom is over the drawing room, but the rest of the bedrooms, being smaller, are set back into the roof. The result of this is a consciously unpretentious elevation, which seems mostly to be made up of a great barn-like roof, into which a multitude of dormers have been let in. All this carries smoothly through until we get to the staff wing. The three storey gable of this set back

THE NEW SURREY STYLE

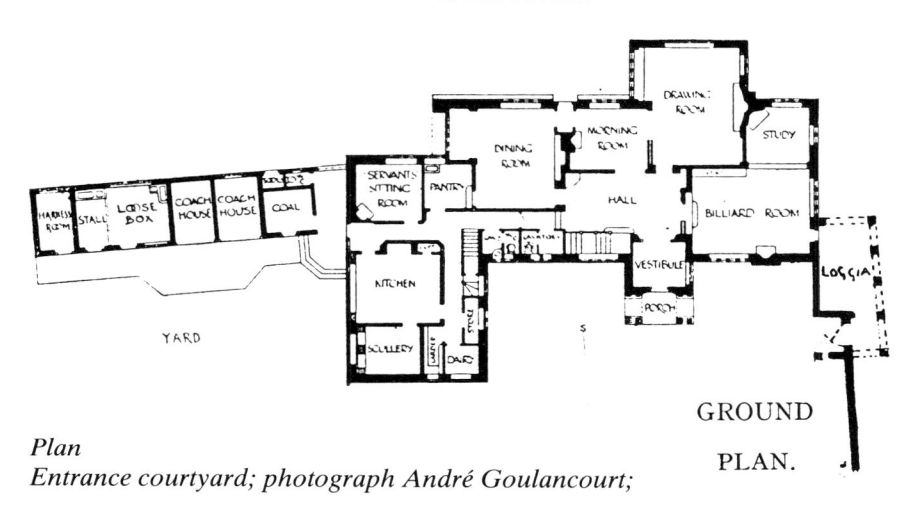

GROUND PLAN.

Plan
Entrance courtyard; photograph André Goulancourt;

wing crashes happily into the gable end of the main roof, the two are seemingly unrelated - even the cill levels to the windows are different. It all seems rather arbitrary at first but it is of course designed not only to further reduce the formality of the elevation, but also to make clear the hierarchy of the rooms within; the service area is clearly demarcated from the rest of the

THE SURREY STYLE

Garden Frontage; André Goulancourt

house. At the same time, with this clash of gables Turner has been able to suggest that the house was built at different times, the service wing being possibly the older house. This is in fact emphasised by the plan, where it can be seen that the service block is a straightforward rectangle with the east facing window of the dining room, designed to catch the morning sun, brought forward to the service wing.

Orchards, Godalming

Orchards is an exact contemporary to Westbrook; it was Lutyens' first sizeable house, coming immediately after Gertrude Jekyll's Munstead Wood. It came as a direct result of Munstead, since the clients, Sir William and Lady Chance, saw Munstead being built and immediately commissioned Lutyens to design their own house nearby. Orchards is the first major Lutyens masterpiece, and is one of the finest houses designed in the Surrey vernacular style.

By 1899, although he was still only 30, Lutyens was completely at home in the Surrey accretive style and Orchards shows the style at its very best. It also shows the way in which it is possible to design very much grander buildings in this style than can ever be envisaged by a study of Nevill's cottages.

Orchards is a big house, which was carefully designed for the special needs of the Chances. Lady Chance was a sculptress of some talent (her delightful garden ornaments are still to be found in many a Surrey garden) and Sir William was a writer; they were also rich. So as well as the usual living rooms, ten bedrooms: a studio and two studies were needed. In addition there was an enormous service wing without which no Edwardian hostess could function. Lutyens solved these complex planning problems by designing the house around a courtyard, with a wing containing a carriage house and stables looking like a barn sticking out on the entrance front.

The planning is straightforward. The services are placed on the east and run in a long wing, from the stables on the north down the whole side of the building, culminating logically with the dining room, which is in the main southern wing. Across the head of the courtyard runs a block with a staff flat to the east and the large north-lit studio to the west; this is linked by a long covered way to the main body of the house, looking onto a small garden that runs all along the south front. The main terraced gardens with wonderful views are in fact to the east, but Lutyens, probably at the suggestion of Gertrude Jekyll, has turned the main rooms of the house away from the view. By making the view a special event, to be seen only by going outside,

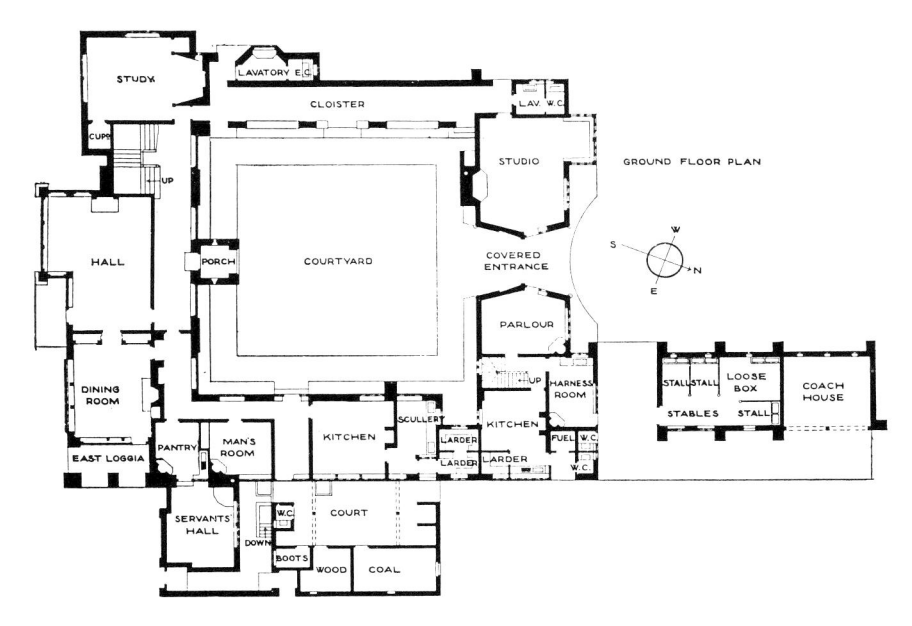

Plan of ground floor; from Lawrence Weaver: Houses and Gardens by E. Lutyens (1913)

the house and garden become a much more unifed entity. This mixing of indoors and outdoors was an essential part of what Jekyll and Lutyens had created at Munstead.

The house is built of Bargate stone, with tall red brick chimneys and red tile-hung gables, kin to so many of Nevill's farmhouses. Indeed the whole complex is designed as if it were a superior manor farm, with its working buildings clustered around the farm yard. It is interesting to compare this with Vann. At Vann Caroë turned a farmyard complex into a house, here Lutyens has suggested a farmyard when building a new house.

Like an ordinary farmhouse, the entrance is understated. The drive is without any gates, open and quite close to the road from Munstead to Shalford, then of course just a lane. The short drive curves up to the buttressed barn attached to the main building that we have already noted, a very unpretentious prelude to a great house. Notice the way in which the roof of this barn runs through in a seemingly unbroken line, because the three dormers punched into it are small they seem to emphasise the solidity of the roof, as does the abrupt way in which it begins with a wholly stone gable whose flat face is broken only with a high hay door, with two small windows to either side.

Entrance elevation; drawn by the author

Weaver: 'Way to stable yard on left and to courtyard on right'

At the end of this barn, and at right angles to it, another long wing runs. At the join a tall but ordinary red brick chimney rises. Beside it a small gable window is tucked in. Then the roof runs in an unbroken line until at the end there is a gablet that develops into a hip and from here the roof sweeps down almost to the ground.

The Bargate stone wall in the centre is angled back on both sides to form an opening which leads into the main court. This entrance is an extraordinarily clever affair for not only does the angle welcome you in, but above there is a small dormer which opens not into a room but into the roof space over the entrance, its sole purpose to lighten what might otherwise be a slightly gloomy entrance. To the right, beyond this there is a high window (which was added later) and then a great two storied oak mullioned bay with a hipped tile roof over, which is placed in exactly the position, and has the right weight, to balance the barn wing on the left. This is the north light to the studio, the chimneys of which we can see poking up just above the roof.

Porch entrance; drawn by the author

Within the courtyard the logic of the plan becomes apparent. To the front is the half-timbered entrance porch (the only half-timbering in the house) at first floor a long strip of leaded windows run under the eaves, representing the wide first floor passage: There are no living rooms looking onto this courtyard, and this is reflected in the fact that there are no large windows here. To the left the service wing runs back, whilst on the right is an open arcade of wide sweeping arches, forming a covered way to Lady Chance's studio and linking directly with her study in the main house.

Garden elevation; drawn by author

André Goulancourt: South front

The south front is a masterly display of asymmetrical balance. Taking this garden front from left to right, on the left the roof sweeps down from a gable to just above the study window, and from this a pair of linked tile-hung dormer windows rise, the cill of the left higher than that of the right. The right hand dormer in fact forms a small bay which lights part of the staircase. Beyond this and set back on a stone wall rise a pair of tall chimneys, exaggerated versions of many a chimney shown in Nevill. Then a gabled stone bay projects making a contrast, in its solid stonework, to the lightness of the first set of gables. In this bay the lower windows light the drawing room, and the upper the main bedroom. The form of every gable is different and here whilst the drawing room windows are a horizontal strip between buttresses, the bedroom windows are taller in two sets of frames. Beyond this wing the eaves of the roof run in a straight line above the heads of the first floor windows, below at the end a series of arches look out over the first of the garden terraces - the arches acting as an artful negative termination to the facade.

Above, the roof line, Lutyens' Surrey-bred understanding of how to balance the horizontals of the roof with the tall verticals of chimneys comes into play. The main chimney of this front comes exactly one third of the way along the facade and is exactly twice the height of the wall from the ground to the eaves. In addition there are a whole series of chimneys riding above the roof. The pair of chimneys to the front is reflected to the left in another identical pair on the other side of the ridge, which in turn are repeated in a group of four similar chimneys to the right. Beyond these there is a further pair, at the end of the building and turned at right angles to all the others. These, when you come round the building, are paired with another set. Behind them a great roof flows, on the top of which and at right angles to it we suddenly find a rectangular chimney of quite a different shape and pattern to any of the others. It is in fact the kitchen chimney and becomes a stop and key to the whole complex series of vertical forms which so perfectly balance the low horizontality of the roof. Take away these chimneys, as has happened in other houses, such as Branksome Hilders, and the movement and lightness of this skilful architecture is maimed and made dumpy.

There is not a detail in Orchards that cannot be found in Nevill's simple vernacular cottages, but here they are transformed by Lutyens into something very much greater than all the parts.

Plate ix

Fulbrook House, South Front. Photographed by André Goulancourt

Plate x

(top) Fulbrook, entrance frontage in c.1910
(below) Fulbrook, swimming pool extension 1975. The half-pipe balustrade in the foreground is continued into the swimming pool extension to form a clerestory.

Plate xi

Tancreds Ford: (top) The garden front, new roofs of the garages to the right. (below) The roof of the new garages sweeping into Falkner's original building. Photographs by the author

Plate xii

The octagonal staircase tower and arch to garage; new games room is to the left. (below) Detail of rustication on voussoir

six

ADDITIONS TO ACCRETIVE HOUSES

By their nature houses in the accretive style are the simplest to add to for obvious reasons. However it is important even here that the original architect's intentions are recognised, so that there is not too much contrast in the use of materials. I give two examples of additions by myself to Surrey houses, one by Harold Falkner, the other by Lutyens, where I have made every effort to follow the style of the original house. It must however be said that this was not Lutyens' own invariable practice, and I give two examples where Lutyens later added to his own houses in a completely different style but, since he was the architect to the original house and the additions, there is an inevitable cohesiveness here that one would not find in the work of a different architect of another generation.

FULBROOK HOUSE

Lutyens and additions by Roderick Gradidge

Fulbrook was built by Lutyens in 1897, just after Munstead Wood of 1896, but a year or so before Orchards. It uses exactly the same materials as Orchards, Bargate stone, red brick chimneys and red tile hanging, but it must be said that it is not so successful as either Munstead or Orchards, although Ian Nairn in *Surrey* buildings of England describes the west front as "a superb composition, two tile-hung gables balancing a big square chimney stack, the horizontal rhythms maintained by the outward sweep at the foot of each stretch of tile hanging." Fulbrook shows Lutyens grappling with the problems of adapting cottages and farmhouses to the scale of a country house; he does not always get it right as he would two years later at Orchards. Added to this he decided at Fulbrook to experiment with a classical interior within this 16th century style house.

The drive approaches from the east and north, coming up past a stable block (see the following chapter, p.125) and then past the sweeping roofs of the northern back quarters of the house, before it swings into the west facing entrance court. This is a formal place with a two storey porch between two wings. The roof of the wing to the left sweeps down almost to the ground. On the right hand an oak and leaded window wraps around the gable end. From this the ground floor is extended and a roof swings up past the gable to another roof which runs behind and parallel to the wing. An octagonal turret is let into this roof. This is an important part of the overall design of the facade, everything seems to revolve around this turret, but in fact it was an afterthought, only added whilst the house was building, when another lavatory was needed! Beyond the turret the facade suddenly changes scale, as if implying that the house was built at different times. A pair of bay windows rise to a roof whose eaves are much higher than the eaves of the rest of the house here - a device that should prepare us for a larger scale facade round the corner.

When we turn the corner this new scale takes over, giving the main front a surprisingly gawky effect. To each end of the facade there are tile-hung gables, though these seem to bear little relationship to what is going on below them. Towards the middle the facade drops back to make a deep recess, lined on both sides with oak mullioned windows; in the centre of this recess another oak mullioned bay projects. The roof is held up on struts which curve out across the bays. This detail is quite common in Kentish yeomen's houses, but Nevill in fact shows a cottage at Compton, a village quite close to Fulbrook, which uses these recessed bays with struts. However all these buildings are very much smaller in scale than Fulbrook, Lutyens' sense of scale seems here to have let him down.

Fulbrook fell on hard times in the 1950s, and was interfered with and altered, a last indignity being its purchase by developers who obtained planning permission (it was unlisted at the time) to build a fifty bedroom wing for a health farm in the garden. Fortunately this came to nothing. In the mid 1970s the house was bought by a European businessman who wished to live in it as a family home and could afford to restore it.

Originally no one had realised the importance of the house, and the intention was to sweep away many of the interior walls, including the classical columns in the drawing room, creating one enormous open plan room on the ground floor. A covered swimming pool was to be built on the east side (the side praised by Ian Nairn), to a design looking rather like a 'modern' school, with enormous sliding glass windows and a flat roof with a fascia four foot six inches deep which was to contain the air extraction and air conditioning equipment. For all this work consent had been obtained! The footings to the pool had already been dug, and inside the house many of the walls had been broken through, when the Victorian Society was approached for their advice and I was asked to become consultant architect for the alterations.

I suggested that rather than continue with the modern design for the pool it would be possible to repeat the great oak and leaded windows, the tiled gables and the sweeping roofs of the Lutyens house, replacing the deep fascia, flat roof and sheets of glass of the 'modern' design, and this was approved with delight. It was of course necessary to fit the new elevations both to Lutyens' details and also to the footings that had already been dug. Work could not be delayed, but since all the materials we wanted to use were local, and the details were already in the house, it did not prove difficult for the builders to continue with building work without any delays.

It is often claimed that it is not possible to reproduce traditional details because they are too expensive. This is quite untrue, modern design is in fact often more expensive than traditional building, since it uses experimental materials in large sheets. In this case the new traditional design, using materials in the same sizes and quality as Lutyens' originals, which included great oak columns supporting the bays, proved to be no more expensive, and much easier to build. All the air conditioning equipment was hidden in the new tiled roof. A barbecue was shown on the original scheme and so this was accommodated, the main pool roof forming a hip at the end here, and the barbecue chimney gave an opportunity for a large red brick stack in the Lutyens' Surrey manner, which acts as a stop to the elevation.

The treatment of the rear was somewhat more complex, for here the roofs had to meld with Lutyens' sweeping roofs on the east front. There was a flat lawn in front of the pool, and at the northern edge there was a tall retaining wall, capped with a typical Lutyens/Surrey detail, half pipe tiles laid horizontally across the top of the wall to form a light decorative screen. This wall was retained, and became the back wall of the swimming pool, with the screen of pipes glazed to give clerestory lighting. The new roof comes down onto this wall and at the rear it sweeps down to almost ground level, stopped at one end by the tall barbecue chimney and at the other by a pair of hipped roofs for the garages. Since the tiled hips and gables followed Lutyens' design, the new work seems to combine well with the original; the pool house itself was linked by an open covered way to the main house, but it reads visually as one.

TANCREDS FORD, TILFORD

Harold Falkner and Roderick Gradidge

Tancreds Ford was built in 1913, and designed by Harold Falkner, Gertrude Jekyll's godson, friend of Lutyens and the architect who largely recreated Farnham. Built for a doctor on the eve of the Great War, it would at the time, have been considered a relatively small house.

Numberless examples of these composed and crafted houses exist from the first fifteen years of our century. Today they still represent most people's ideal house.

During the Edwardian autumn, the vernacular revival style had developed, largely under Lutyens' influence, into what is labelled Neo-Georgian, but might better be called (if it were not such a mouthful) Georgian-vernacular-revival. The style owes as much to the vernacular revival as it does to copy-book Georgian architecture, specifically in the way in which natural materials are always insisted on, whilst symmetry is by no means always strictly adhered to. Nonetheless the classical detailing of such things as door cases and cornices was always entirely correct. Between the wars this was an almost universal Anglo-Saxon style; in America it is called Colonial Revival. Sitting happily, and without apology in town and country, beside architecture of any period and without forcing itself on to its surroundings, it was a style that was as serviceable for banks, shops and railway stations as it was for houses. Needless to say the builder's Neo-Georgian of today bears little relation to this style.

Tancreds Ford is typical of this style. The garden front is formal, there is a central colonnade and to either side two stumpy wings project forward under hipped roofs. On one side a long service wing tails off. The entrance front shows surprisingly little attempt at symmetry, or rather a symmetrical front has been broken by the way in which a new and asymmetrical wing seems to have been put down in front of the original. In the putative centre of the facade there is a Georgian door case, to either side is rusticated brickwork, which runs up to form a frontispiece. To either side of this are symmetrically placed casement windows, two to the right, but on the left, immediately after the first set of windows, the new wing juts forward, demarcated by a tall rusticated brick chimney. The eaves here are at the cill level of the first floor windows, and in this manner the fact that it is the kitchen wing is clearly indicated. In the roof of the main block a series of dormers are formally placed, though there is an additional dormer, lower than the others which breaks the pattern and accentuates the informal elements in the elevation.

Tancreds Ford has always been a private house, and it was bought in the early 1980s by a writer who commissioned me to alter it to suit his working needs. It was decided that the whole of the upper floor should be made into a library and writing room. This was accomplished with considerable alterations to the roof structure, but with no obvious effect on the external elevations, except that a small balcony was formed in the place of the dormer on the garden elevation; below is a new Diocletian lunette, which was formed to give more light in the upper part of the vaulted hall.

The use of the attic for the library meant that a large number of bedrooms had to be done away with, and more bedroom space was now needed. In addition to this the garages were badly placed and large cars could not be parked inside them. So it was decided to link the garage with the main house, extend this and form a new set of garages facing outwards from the house down the back drive, linking the two buildings together with a series of sweeping tiled hipped roofs. In this way we made room in the new roof spaces for three further bedrooms suites.

On the entrance front this formed an enlarged open court, with the new bedroom wing, with a games room under, coming forward of the main block. In the angle between the blocks an octagonal turret was formed for a secondary staircase, beside it there is an arch. This turret and arch gave an opportunity for some suitable architectural detail. On his house Harold Falkner had rusticated each corner in contrasting red bricks. One of these rusticated corners occurred at the position of the new arch. So this rustication was carried round the arch, forming voussoirs. The 'keystone', which thrusts up into the passage windows above, is made from tiles laid vertically

This two coloured brick rustication, when carried around the Octagonal tower, led to some difficulties for the brick manufacturer and the bricklayer, but they overcame them in a craftsmanly way without having to consult anyone. The same thing occurred with the highly complex roof that had developed. This three dimensional form was laid out on the site, and a satisfactory solution arrived at without too much difficulty. Since these additions were designed and built in a completely traditional manner they presented only the kind of difficulties that a well trained builder can readily overcome, and he of course enjoys setting his ingenuity to solving such problems, a fact not usually true of fashionable modern materials and designs.

The new roof was tiled in second hand tiles to match the existing and it was possible to find from local brickworks bricks that matched the original bricks in colour. It was of course necessary to have special bricks fired, since all bricks today are in metric sizes, and a satisfactory coursing can never be achieved between imperial and metric sizes.

*

A note on the metric system

This matter of the metric system bedevils all work of addition to old buildings. All old buildings were built to imperial sizes, and even if these sizes were not to be preferred in building works it is of course essential that all visible work should be made to fit with what already exists. The metric equivalent is not near enough, there are often discrepancies of as much as three quarters of an inch in these equivalents. The recent metrification forced on the building trade is both expensive and ultimately destructive to old buildings; soon no materials in Imperial measure will be available and it will become necessary for all elements such as doors and windows put in old buildings to be specially made.

There is a further important element in this relationship between metric and imperial dimensions. If an addition to an old building is built in metric dimensions it will inevitably not sit well with the original building, since all the sizes will be slightly out. Nowadays all buildings are measured for bills of quantities in metric, drawings have to be drawn metric, yet drawings for additions should always be designed and dimensioned in the old measurements, with the correct metric size, not the metric equivalent, figured beside them.

It is also worth pointing out that old buildings should not be measured with a metric measure, since this also leads to inaccurate dimensioning. Far too often in surveys dimensions of buildings that have been built to the imperial measure are shown in metric round figures, and this can lead to what may well become expensive errors or bodges when the dimensions are translated to the reality of the building site.

*

RUCKMANS, OAKWOOD PARK

Edwin Lutyens

Metrification was not something that affected Lutyens when he made his two additions to Ruckmans. The first addition came very early in his career in 1894, but he was called in again in 1902, when he added a music room.

Ruckmans was a line of three cottages, tile-hung with a half hipped gable. These Lutyens left almost intact, but to the front of them he built what amounts to a new house, leaving the original cottages to become the entrance and staircase hall. The new extension is brave and splendid. From the horizontal roofline of the original cottages three gables, three storeys high, jut out, tile-hung from the top of the gables to just over the ground floor windows. This ground floor drops back in places to form a verandah. Each gable juts just a little forward of the wall plane, thus forming a separate bay the ridges of these gables are at the same height as the ridge of the original building, so that the whole addition is completely integrated into the cottages. (see p109 below)

Music room extension, 1902 Country Life

In 1902 Lutyens was asked to add a music room, since it was said that the original cottage rooms were too low to hear music in. Instead of continuing the long roofline of the original cottages, which a less imaginative architect might have considered, Lutyens decided instead to build a completely new room, linked only by a wide passage to the main house. This new tall room is designed in a quite different manner to the original additions, tall sash windows rise up to a hipped roof, giving the impression that an early 18th century orangery has been added to an earlier accretive farmhouse. But whilst the style and character of this elegant little building is very different, it is important to see that Lutyens has been very careful not to dominate his original building. The music room is set away from the main building and, although it is on a much bigger scale than its neighbour, he has been extremely careful to keep down the scale of his elements. The brick and the tiles are of course similar, but notice the way in which Lutyens has used the smallest panes that be possibly could in his sash windows.

This elegant and orangery-like structure might make an excellent exemplar for anyone needing to add a covered swimming pool to an old house. It is not always right to add, as I did at Fulbrook, a large structure which exactly matches the original building; often a building in a dissimilar but related style will give a more satisfactory result.

CROOKSBURY

Edwin Lutyens

The story of Crooksbury stretches from beginning to end of Lutyens' career, from 1889 when he built the original house, the first house of his career, until 1914, when he made his last additions at the very end of the great period of country house building.

The first Crooksbury was a simple enough L shaped house, which he built for Arthur Chapman as a country retreat (see page 80 below). However nine years later Chapman decided to live there permanently and commissioned Lutyens to add a large wing making the house considerably grander. He had designed the original house in a half-timbered vernacular style taken from his master, Ernest George. By 1898 Lutyens had developed his own style, and was at this time moving away from his earlier vernacular style to a more formal Georgian-influenced style. Indeed only the year before he had built his first Georgian style street facade, the Liberal Club in Farnham, for Arther Chapman. So we must expect something very different, and indeed the east elevation of his new wing, which faces away from the earlier house, is the first example of Lutyens' using a classical style in a country house. But this does not mean that he crashes his new work in a different style into the old. In the linking passage where the two wings are seen together, he is extremely careful to create a series of sweeping roofs and tall chimneys which will complement his earlier house.

In 1914, the house was sold and the new owners asked that the east front be altered so that it was closer in style to the rest of the house, though Lutyens rightly did not like doing it. But, as Hussey remarks; "If he would not do it, somebody else would, so rather than let alien hands dismember his first born, he hardened his heart and plunged in the adze himself". Alas his heart was not in it and the result is really very unsatisfactory. Only in his extensions beside his old link, where he devises a splendidly complex series of roof forms over a deep ingle and a bay window which are set against tall chimneys, does he display his absolute mastery of the Surrey style.

ACCRETIVE HOUSES

Crooksbury, garden front, first alteration 1898 (Top)
Crooksbury garden front re-faced 1914 Country Life

PART II

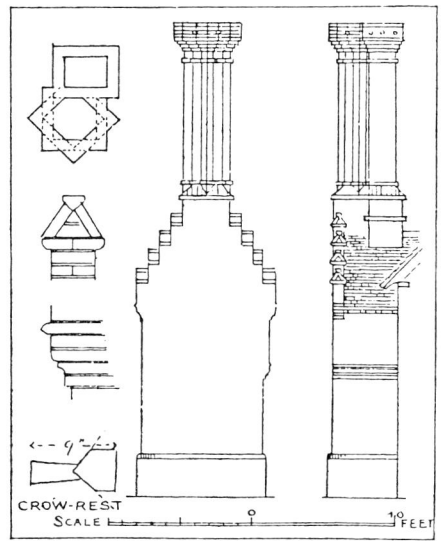

Unstead; detail of chimney; Nevill: (Old Cottages and Domestic Architecture of S.W. Surrey)

seven

DETAILING

In the first part of this book we have been concerned with the overall look of Surrey buildings, now we will consider the traditional details. Detailing gives a building its individuality, something that the arts and crafts, and, to a certain degree Victorian, architects understood well. The books that we have been talking of contained drawings showing details of old buildings, details as useful today as when they first appeared and were studied by arts and crafts architects. In addition to Nevill and Curtis Green, we will be using Arthur J. Penty *The Elements of Domestic Design* (1930 Architectural Press), which has been called "the Grammar of the Vernacular Revival," by Stuart Gray: *Edwardian Architecture* (1985). Penty, like all the other authors, was a practising architect, and used many of his traditional details in a new house that he built not in Surrey but at Ditchling in Sussex. The majority of the details drawn represent variations on vernacular revival standards, they will fit into most Surrey cottages and houses where stone or brick is the main material; half-timbering of course has its own natural vocabulary of forms and detailing.

CHIMNEYS

Visually it is the chimneys of Surrey that one remembers. As Nevill boasts, "although elsewhere more elaborate chimneys may be found on the larger houses, I know of no district where there is so much variety of the humbler kind worthy of close study". Surrey chimneys come in all shapes but only in one size - large. Again and again, both in Nevill's examples or in houses by Lutyens and his contemporaries, it is the great chimneys that dominate the buildings. The chimneys by no means need to match one another, variety of forms was common practice on even quite small houses. What is certainly true is that if even a relatively modern Surrey house, like E.J.May's Branksome Hilders, is shorn of its chimneys, all of its character goes. This is doubly true of old cottages.

It was always said in the early part of the century that, with the advent of central heating and electricity, chimneys had become redundant and it was logical to remove all fireplaces and chimneys. As well as having a disastrous effect on old buildings, this proved to be short sighted. With the new gas log fires, Scandinavian stoves and the refusal of most people to forego the pleasure to be gained from an open fire, chimneys have made a come-back in those houses where they are still usable. So today there is less chance of chimneys being removed and indeed every likelihood of new chimneys being built.

The majority of Surrey chimneys are built of red brick - an almost universal practice from one end of the county to the other. Chimneys in old Surrey buildings used bright red but very thin brick. Nevill insists on this, (*The Builder* 29.IX.1888) "The bricks at Unstead are only 2½ in. thick, and four courses do not make a foot." K.W.E.Gravett, confirms the fact (*Surrey Archaeological Journal* 1966) bricks used in chimneys commonly gave as little as a ten inch rise in four courses.

Gravett points out that chimneys were originally built of brick for fireproofing, but since the early builders were uncertain of the strength of their bricks they did not dare to make them loadbearing, probably because the flue openings were so big. Nevill says that they were as much as 18 inches square. This meant of course that the brick walls, usually only one brick

Cottage at Eashing; Nevill: Old Cottages

DETAILING: CHIMNEYS

thick, were for all that they look so solid, relatively unstable, particularly with the often enormous caps built on top of the chimneys.

Nowadays of course we make our flues much narrower, with the result that we can build much slimmer chimneys, but this means that a purely functional chimney can look too flimsy against the strong horizontality of the roof line. The only way that this can be solved is to retain the flue width but to thicken the flue walls, which will both help the structural stability of the chimney and much improve its look. It is important to the look of a building that any new chimney is built as large as, and in nearly as extravagant a manner as the old chimneys, if it is to look right. At Fulbrook (pl. x), the new chimney on the swimming pool extension is given bulk and character to rival its peers on the house itself.

Usually in old houses the basic chimney plan is rectangular rising from a rectangular base and capped with projecting bricks; Nevill drew such a simple chimney at Shoelands. However such simplicity did not often interest the Surrey chimney builders. Directly a chimney was expected to hold more than one flue then there was an opportunity to take a more plastic approach to chimney design. The first solution might be to build the separate flues next to one another but not on the same plane, as at Shottermill. A more complex example of this treatment is found in the four flues at Ash Manor.

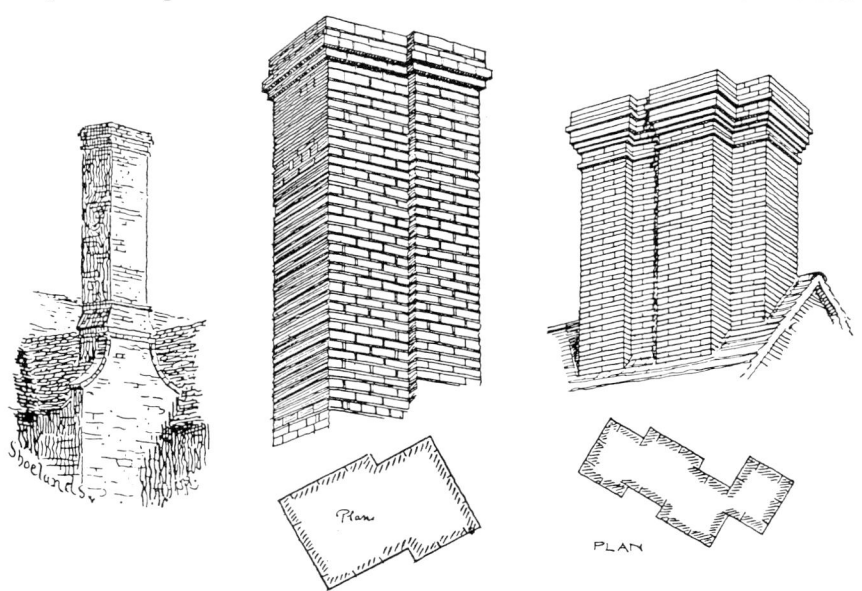

Nevill: Shoelands; Curtis Green: Shottermill, Ash Manor

The trouble with this treatment is that it can give too heavy an outline and so the chimney builders cast about for methods to lighten the bulk. The Haslemere example tries, not entirely successfully, to reduce the bulk by forming the flues into a cross shaped plan; this form can really only work when the chimney is in a central position. The builder of the first example, from Gomshall, has attempted to reduce the weight by separating his flues and running a line of projecting bricks up the centre of each chimney. This is an interim stage to what was to become the standard Surrey chimney, seen at Farncombe and the second one from Gomshall. At Farncombe the two flues are twisted to forty five degrees on plan, with a gap between the chimneys, whilst at Gomshall where there are three flues the central flue is star shaped on plan.

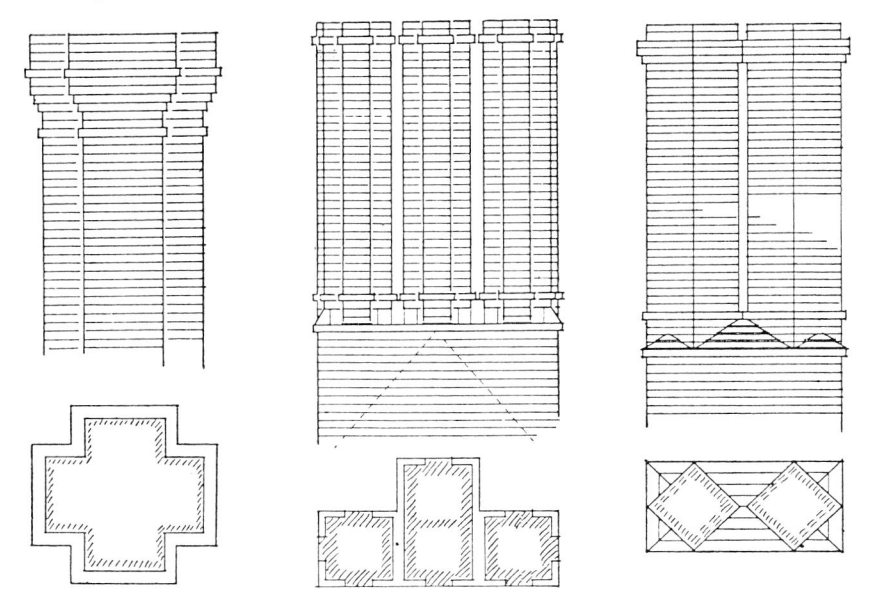

Curtis Green: Haslemere; Gomshall; Farncombe;

This design was developed further in the striking chimney at Rake House, where the two outer flues were square on plan, whereas the central flue is turned forty five degrees. This proved to be a classic form and was copied on numberless occasions by Lutyens and the other architects of the Arts and Crafts Movement. Another favourite type with Lutyens, (as at Bonnet's Farm, Ockley) has both the flues placed at forty five degrees and kept separate with only the thinnest gap between them, just touching at the

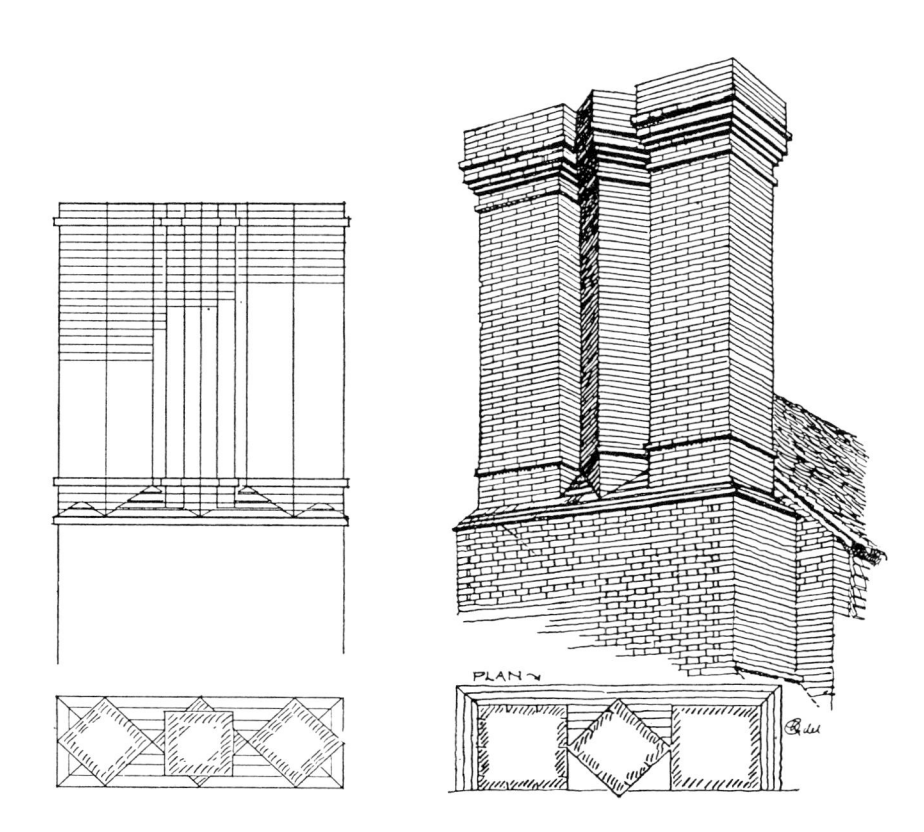

Curtis Green: Rake Manor; Gomshall

surprisingly heavy caps. This is of course in the same manner as the chimney Green shows at Farncombe, but the immensely tall flues of Ockley are more elegant. Lutyens made an almost exact copy of this chimney in the pair at the entrance to Tigbourne Court, (see frontispiece). So enamoured of these twin flues was he that at Tigbourne the two flues on the right serve but one fireplace!

A further elaboration was for the brickwork to the flues to form a star on plan. There seems to have been a sort of hierarchy in chimney forms, and these elaborate, star shaped chimneys as Nevill calls them seem to have been used more often than not over the main fireplace ingle, the solid weight of the ingle contrasting with the spindly elegance of the chimney. An example

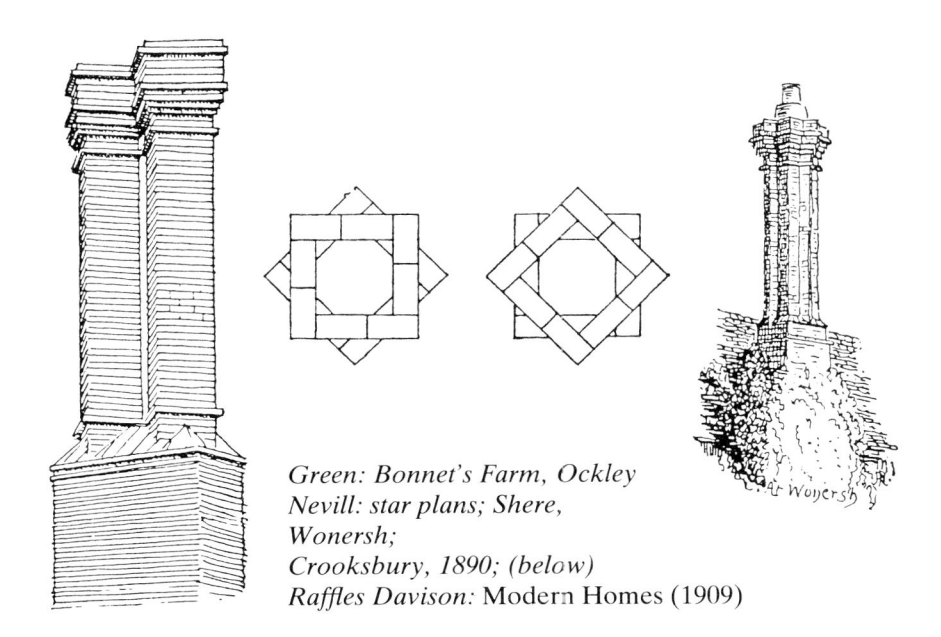

Green: Bonnet's Farm, Ockley
Nevill: star plans; Shere,
Wonersh;
Crooksbury, 1890; (below)
Raffles Davison: Modern Homes (1909)

of this can be seen in the house at Shere (see page 53.) Lutyens copied it for his first important house, Crooksbury. Note the way in which Lutyens follows the hierarchy of chimneys. The tall plain chimney to the left serves the kitchen, whilst the small chimney over the porch merely serves a fireplace in the hall. This hierarchy is also echoed in the treatment of the walls, the main living quarters are half-timbered (not a finish much used by Lutyens later in his career), whilst the servants wing is tile-hung in the manner of a cottage.

Plate xiii

Helen Allingham: An Old Surrey Cottage. *Reproduced by permission of Marley plc*

Plate xiv

Tigbourne: detail of galletted wall

Plate xv

Tigbourne: balcony detail. Photographs by author

Plate xvi

Helen Allingham: Cottage at Witley. *Reproduced by permission of Marley plc*

DETAILING: CHIMNEYS

ROOFS
Roof Structure
This is not the place for a discussion on the design of traditional roof timbers, indeed this has now become an area of specialist study. *English Historic Carpentry* by Cecil A. Hewett (Phillimore 1980) can be recommended for further study in this matter. A specialist should be called in if the alteration of an obviously old roof is contemplated. Although Surrey

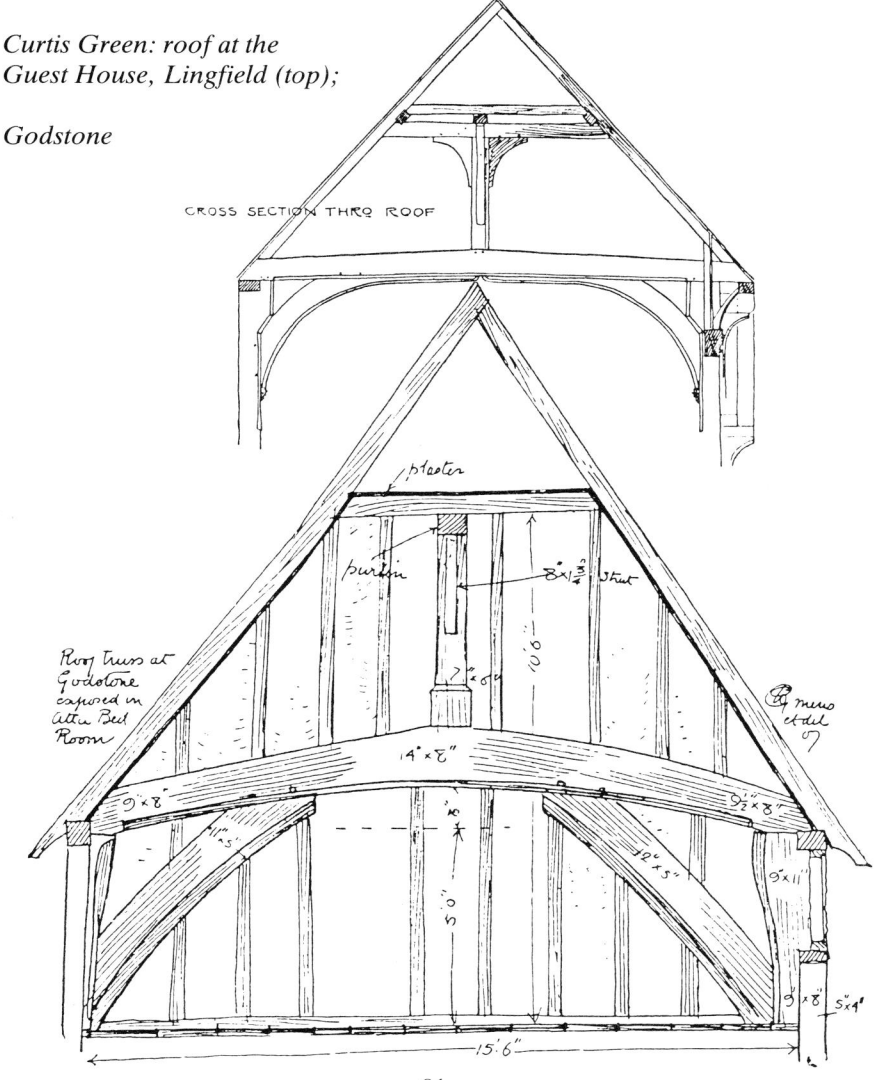

Curtis Green: roof at the Guest House, Lingfield (top);

Godstone

boasts some good medieval timber roofs they are of such little importance nationally that Hewett hardly mentions any Surrey buildings in his comprehensive and authoritative book.

Nonetheless Baily in 1863, with his specific interest in Surrey half-timbered houses, Nevill and Curtis Green all show examples of fine roof trusses from Surrey hall houses, and it must be remembered that the majority of what we think of as 'cottages' that have survived until today were originally 'hall' houses. The roofs at Godstone and Lingfield, as well as Great Tangley (see page 38) are variants on the king post principle, but using a collar beam. This collar beam is supported on a strutted king post, which in turn is supported by a large strutted tie beam. It seems that quite often in Surrey, unlike for instance Suffolk, these trusses were not intended to be seen, a plaster ceiling being run under the main tie beam. Although this would seem not to be so at Great Tangley, where the trusses are decoratively chamferred, although, as we have seen, even here a later floor was fitted in above the hall.

Roofing Materials

Just as the great majority of Surrey chimneys are made of red brick, so the great majority of the old Surrey roofs that we see today are of hand made red tiles. In fact these tiles are of relatively recent date, having been originally brought in from Holland in the 16th century, but it was not long before they were fired within the county, and from that time on they replaced thatch. In 1908 Curtis Green wrote that thatch was fast disappearing in Surrey, both because it was dangerous because of fire (he says it was whitewashed in the 14th century as a precaution against this) but also because even then straw was becoming unusable because of machine reaping. No doubt to the regret of such artists as Helen Allingham who loved to draw thatch. Lutyens built a thatched potting shed for Gertrude Jekyll at Munstead Wood. The thatch was created from hoop-chips, an unlikely but it is said traditional form of Surrey thatch, which was a by-product of the local wooden barrel-hoop industry, an example of Jekyll's knowledge and interest in the proper use of old crafts.

Green continues: "Roofs of Horsham stone slates are often found in Surrey; the slates are laid in diminishing courses, the big ones at the eaves and the smallest at the apex of the roof." They were held on by wood pegs, over the years these rotted and the roofs needed to be relaid. He goes on to say, "no doubt when these removals took place the stone was replaced by tiles." Since 1908 this seems to have become almost universal, nowadays stone roofs are quite rare in Surrey.

Cottages at Ockley; Surrey Local Studies Library, Guildford

Roof Forms.

The form of the roof is basic to the massing of any building, even if as Nevill states: "The original roofs of cottages were, as I have said, generally perfectly plain, and the lean-tos that form such picturesque masses are therefore to great extent the result of accident." Any additions should be made to conform in one way or another to this sense of 'happy accident'.

Penty analyses how the roofs of simple rectangular buildings can be added to. He starts with the simplest of lean-tos in Figure 1, and ends with a relatively complex series of hips. Where in Figure 1 the lean-to breaks from the eaves, giving an uncomfortable junction with the gable, in Figure 2 the roof is run up to create a hipped end. Note the change of pitch between the lean-to and the main roof. Figure 3 shows a double storey addition, but since it is narrower on plan the ridge of the extension is lower than the main roof, thus making a demarcation between the old and the new.

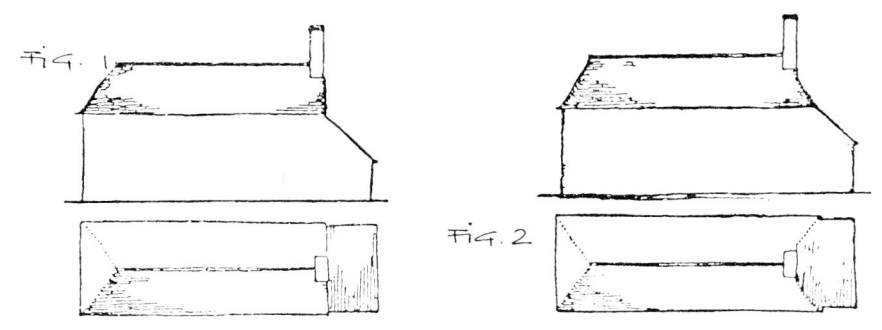

Figure 4 shows how unsatisfactory the extension to the right is when fractionally longer than the original. The greater strength of the shorter but higher left hand wing has equal weight, because of its heavy double hipped roof, with the longer but lower right hand wing, which causes a duality. Figures 5 and 6 show a much better solution. Here although the extensions are as long as, or, in 6, longer than the original, the main house is allowed to dominate. In one case the roof is extended. with a lean-to and in 6, with a series of gable-ended extensions each with a lower ridge. 7 and 8 show this theme continued with more satisfactory hipped ends. Notice the way the central, large chimney plays an important part in examples 5, 6 and 7.

Figures 9, 10, 11, 12 and 13 show how best to handle short wings using lean-tos and hips. The treatment of l0 is somewhat eccentric. Here a narrow gabled roof runs into a lean-to which in its turn runs into the gable end wall, but since the extension is not quite long enough two small hips are formed before the gable is met. The resulting clash is not entirely satisfactory.

Figure 14 shows lean-tos at either end of a simple rectangular gabled roof. The resulting symmetry can often be very satisfactory as long as it does not look forced. 15 shows the combination of a lean-to and a gable, created by a wing that runs back from the main block. Notice the way in which the ridge of the wing is slightly higher than the original building. Right angled ridges running through level always seem to be avoided, probably because in this manner each wing is clearly defined.

Figure 16 shows a fairly complex roof form. In the first plan the main rectangle has been widened to the rear and one side, with the main roof carried down as a lean-to to cover this. Notice the way in which a lean-to roof has been avoided on the short end elevation. The roof of the extension has been hipped back up to the eaves, thus reflecting the hip of the original roof which gives a more finished effect. The final example takes this detail further. Here the main body is as wide as the hipped extension, and the main

Fig. 3

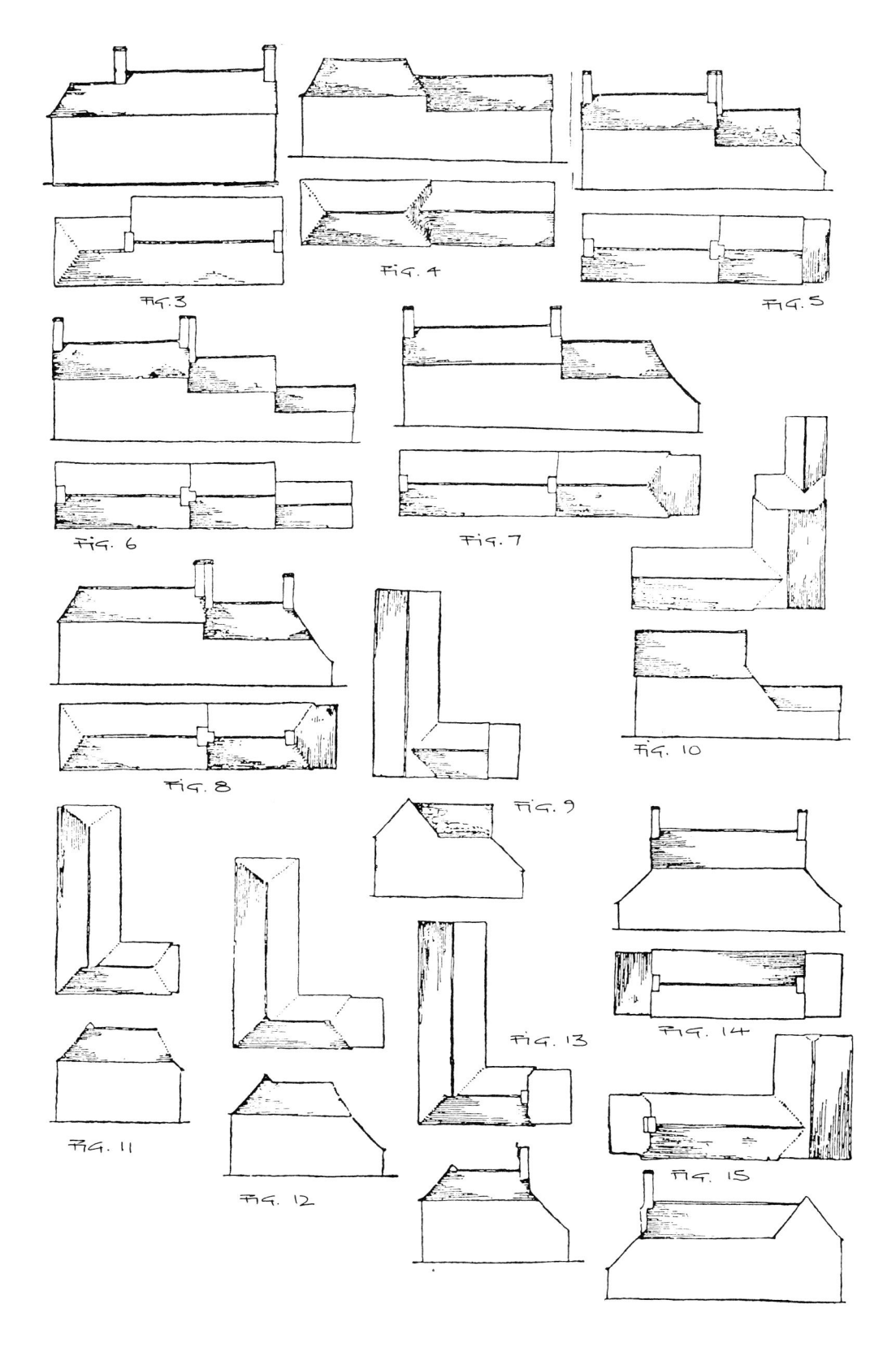

Fig. 4

Fig. 5

Fig. 6

Fig. 7

Fig. 8

Fig. 9

Fig. 10

Fig. 11

Fig. 12

Fig. 13

Fig. 14

Fig. 15

THE SURREY STYLE

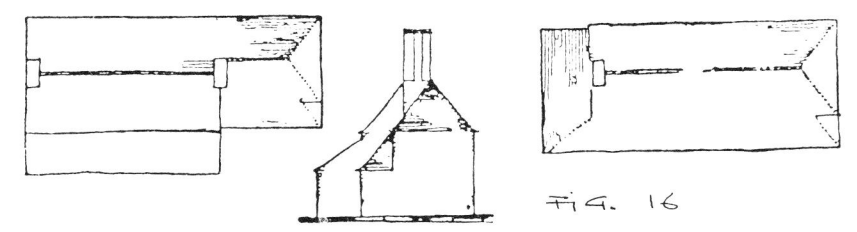

FIG. 16

block is extended with a lean-to. The position of the large chimney is all important, for it is round this vertical element that all the horizontal roofs pivot.

Of course in reality roofs do not exactly follow Pentys' formalised schemes. Proffits Farm has a thatched lean-to added not to the back or side, but to the front, and this makes a neat enclosure to the garden. Such plan

Proffits Farm, Walton-on-the-Hill, 1890; Surrey Local Studies Library

was rare in older cottages; however it was popular for the small architect-designed cottages of the inter-war years in the new towns, such as Letchworth or Welwyn, or in the superior suburbs of North Surrey, at such places as Walton-on-the-Hill, where, ironically, this cottage was demolished in 1907 and was very likely replaced by just such a suburban home.

A more traditional form of roof is found on Hurst Manor House, Worplesdon. Once again the wing comes forward of the main part of the house, but here it is a straightforward gabled wing. But note that neither the eaves or the ridge runs through at the same level. At the rear there is a single storey extension.

Hurst Farm, 1911; Surrey Local Studies Library

A rear view of the roofs of Gomshall photographed in 1890 shows a whole series of different ridge lines and gables, representing a riot of happy accidents. Oddly enough there is only one lean-to; one would expect to see more at the back of a village street; this is no doubt due to the fact that the ground rises steeply. It cannot have been that pleasant backing on to the pond which might flood in winter or become stagnant in the summer, the rear extensions were accordingly unimportant.

Gomshall, Surrey Local Studies Library 1890.

One of the most complex examples of the use of traditional roof forms can be seen in E.J.May's Ballindune built in 1905, an example of an Edwardian accretive design. May has devised a highly complex plan. The main part of the house faces south east with the dining room and a loggia forward of the main block. The entrance is from the east, and a separate hipped roof billiard-room block, preferred by Edwardian convention to be separated from the main house, thrusts out diagonally, running parallel with the curve of the drive. A large coach house block, cross shaped on plan, is rather eccentrically, though logically, placed in front of the entrance, linked to the main house with a porch.

The way in which May manages to roof these complex plans in a completely un-forced manner shows the sophistication that had been reached at the turn of the century by designers in this three-dimensional art form. On the left the coachman's cottage rises in a broad gable, to either side of it a roof, which covers the main stable block, is hipped up. From this, beside the tall broad chimney to the coachman's parlour, a low wing runs off to form the porch for the entrance to the main part of the house. Notice how the walls angle in here, a trick that May has picked up from Lutyens' Orchards.

DETAILING: ROOFS

The ridge of the roof of the main house, hipped at both ends, runs through in one line, broken only by a higher wing that runs at right angles in the centre. This both demarcates the front door and covers the projecting dining room wing on the south. At the front door itself the half hipped gabled and tile-hung wing corbels out, but otherwise the main wall to the house is very plain; the only windows are a band right up under the eaves, which light the gallery to the two storied hall. The hipped roof of the billiard room, with a ridge at the same level as the eaves of the main house, is allowed to run into the corner of the block. What could have been an unfortunate joint is masked by May by a tall chimney.

May, like Lutyens, understands how to handle his multitude of disparate chimneys. Each is to a different design, though they all follow Surrey precedent, and although they all come quite logically where one would expect them on the plan, they none the less are absolutely essential to the balance of the whole three dimensional scheme.

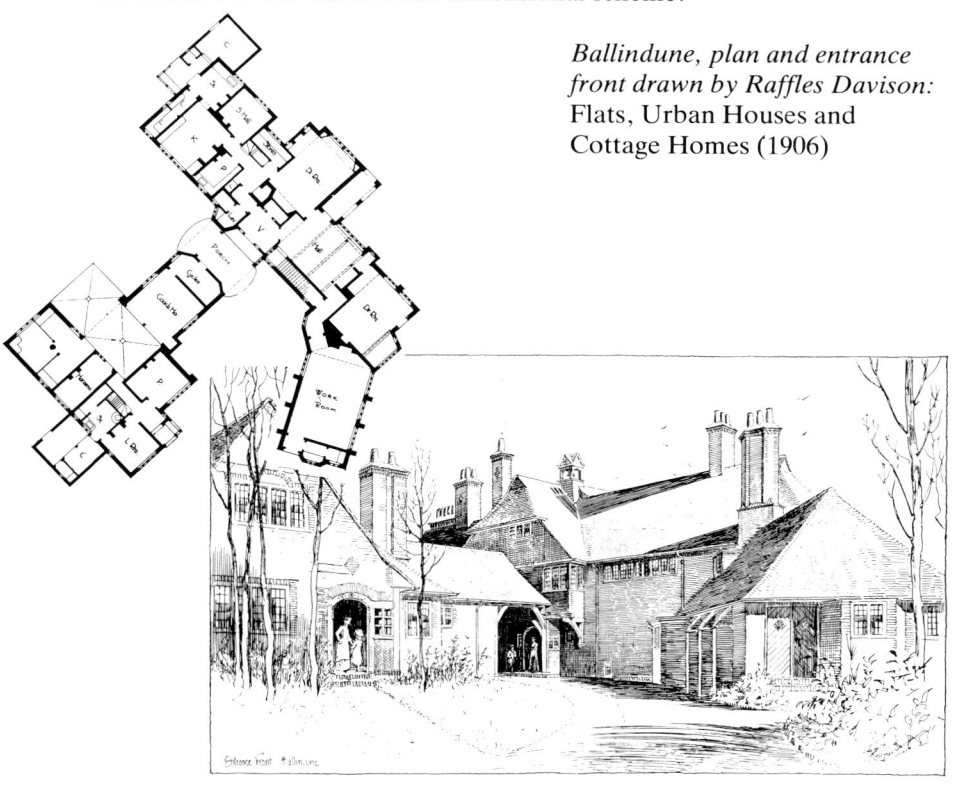

Ballindune, plan and entrance front drawn by Raffles Davison: Flats, Urban Houses and Cottage Homes (1906)

Nursecombe Bramley; Nevill: Old Cottages

GABLES

The gable is the most common way in which the long line of the roof is broken, either to end a wing, or else to form a complete room in an attic roof space. For this reason it is almost unknown for a gable that runs along the wall line not to have a window in it, though of course on the end of a wing

Munstead Wood; Raffles Davison: Modern Homes, (1909)

DETAILING: GABLES

windowless gables are quite common.

An example of a pair of gables on the front face of a cottage in Nursecombe has a well handled roof; from the left a lean-to roof is brought down and hipped round the front of the house. Whilst the eaves of the gables are very low, they do not come down to the line of the eaves of the main roof; it is this that gives them their own importance, if the eaves had run through the elevation would have developed a sentimental blandness.

Lutyens' design for Munstead Wood is very similar. Once again the roof runs through in a straight line and on the right there is a pair of gables that takes up most of that part of the facade. Lutyens' is of course the more sophisticated design, note that the ridge of the gable and roof are not on the same line, and the gables themselves are broader and the gable eaves come down almost to the main eaves.

It is Lutyens' chimneys that make Munstead, and in particular the great chimney that supports the left hand gable, perfectly balancing it against the long roof line to the left. It is remarkable that a young architect of only twenty-seven could handle these Surrey dorms with such sophistication, but then he had known these Surrey cottages since he was a young boy, and instead of going away to school like most of his contemporaries, had wandered the villages and farms around his home of Thursley. Nursecombe by bicycle is no distance at all from Munstead.

Gables can of course come in all shapes and sizes, sometimes dominating a whole facade, as with the house at Farncombe, which is no more than a single gable supported by two lean-tos.

House at Farncombe; Nevill: Old Cottages

Lucas Green Manor has a main facade made up of a long roof, stopped at each end by two gables. The roof carries on beyond the west gable to form a smaller roof, at the same ridge level but with higher eaves, which covers an hexagonal half-timbered bay which runs up the whole of the west front of the house. It is rare to see this detail in the 16th century, but it was much used at the end of the 19th century and in the builders' semis of the 1930s.

Lucas Green Manor, West End; Surrey C.C.

The pictures of Osbrook's (or Osgood's, or as Green has it Oscroft's or Street's!) Farm at Capel in 1890 and 1908, show it as it was before Lutyens made additions in 1911.

Osbrook's has a rather more complex layout of gables than we have seen before; it also has two show fronts. To the left, two wings project, forming a court with a front door and simple porch; everything on this facade is half-timbered with herringbone brick infill. To the right there is a newer and more extravagant show front, with moulded brick around the windows which would seem to be 16th century in date. The way the gables are handled is of interest. The wing on the extreme left is narrower than that on the right, so the ridge of the gable comes into the roof quite low down. The right hand gable however is allowed to dominate, the ridge is at very nearly the same

DETAILING: GABLES

Oscrofts, Capel in 1890 (top) Surrey Studies Library, Guildford. Oscrofts; Galsworthy Davie in Curtis Green

level as the main roof ridge, and is about two slates higher than the gables to the brick front. As usual no ridge runs through at the same level.

Galsworthy Davie's photograph shows the front around the corner on the right. What is of interest here is the way that the gable on the left is divided by the great chimney breast. The gable seems to run up behind the chimneys to form the ridge that we have already seen. However the base of the chimney is stopped off well below the ridge, with the result that the angled flues partly run up in front of the gable, which gives a rather ungainly effect, and indeed suggests that the gable is stopped behind the chimney with a flat roof. The way that the chimneys, each with a triplet of angled flues, sail over the roofs and dominate the facade is very typical of old Surrey farmhouses. It is interesting to see that the small chimney, photographed in 1890 on the left of the brick facade, has by 1908 blossomed into a full scale Surrey chimney, cutting into the left hand gable.

In a street scene, where more often than not, (before they were smoothed away and made polite with a horizontal cornice by the Georgians), a line of gables of different sizes made a romantic composition. The High Street, Haslemere has a splendid display of gables. As Green draws it the terrace makes a perfectly balanced composition, particularly in the way the line of gables is stopped at one end with a hipped roof, and at the other by a straight wing, topped by a pitched roof. Between this there are three distinct groups. The first set of three butts up to the hipped wing, indeed the last gable is truncated so that the higher eaves on the left may run through with the gable. After the first trio we have one large gable, very slightly jettied out, whose ridge runs back to the main roof, the junction being masked by a large chimney. Beyond this a wing is corbelled out, from Green's drawing seeming to be cantilevered without any supports; this is tile-hung and roofed with two gables. If it were not for the fact that the eaves of these roofs run through with the eaves of the main building one would be

Curtis Green: High Street, Haslemere

tempted to call these large dormer windows. The line between gables and dormers is often a fine one, the trim being exactly the same for both elements.

EAVES AND BARGEBOARDS

Probably the area most prone to damp penetration is the vertical junction between the walls and the horizontal roof. For this reason all traditional building is designed so that the roof projects well over the wall to throw the rain water off. This overthrow is of course much more important where a roof, with its concentrated load of water, comes down over a wall, than it is at a gable end, where rather less overhang is needed. To overcome any drips that there may be here it is common to slightly tilt the tiles up at the gable end, thus throwing the rain back down the roof.

Surrey, being in the mild south east, is a county of plain gable ends. The roof is cut relatively more tightly up against the wall than it would be, say, on the North Yorkshire moors. An overhang of no more than 1½ to 2 inches is quite common, though of course if such neat detailing is to be tried great care must be taken that all rain water is thrown back on to the main roof.

Rear elevation, 25 High St., Guildford; Nevill

The back of the well-known classical facade of 25, High Street, Guildford, is plainer, though it too has mullioned windows and a curved 'Ipswich' bay, much beloved of Norman Shaw. The brickwork runs up to very tightly clipped eaves.

In Church Street, Godalming, a half-timbered front has a gabled frontispiece corbelled out. From this the gable itself is corbelled out again and is tile-hung, the tilework being brought out to the very front. It may be in this case that this represents a repair, the tiling being planted on an old and no longer weather-proof gable. Originally the gable probably looked more like

Nevill; Curtis Green

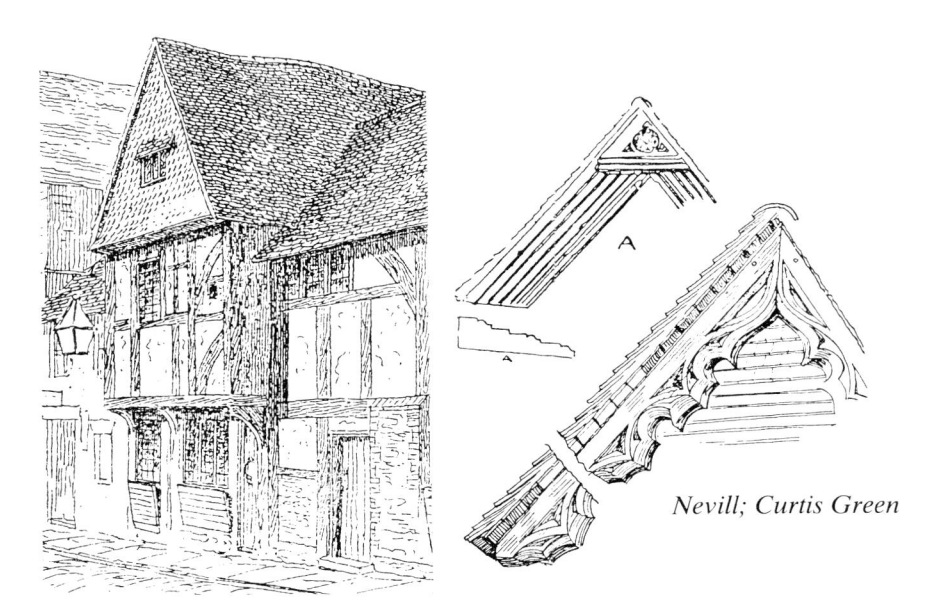

Church Street, Godalming; Nevill

its neighbours.

Elaborate decorative bargeboards, much liked by Victorian water colourists and romantic architects, are not very common in Surrey. If bargeboards were used they would more likely be of the simplest kind, a piece of moulded timber fixed under the eaves, as in Nevill's example. Nevill points out that this was a late development; "At the earlier dates the ends of the joists were generally allowed to show, and it was probably when timber went up in price, as it did very much at this time, (16th century), that the joists became smaller, and the ends were concealed".

The third way of handling gables, and one which certainly belongs to a later period, is the decorative brick gable which is raised above the roof to form a parapet. There are examples of this in Surrey, but once again it cannot be said to be a typical form; it was a style that was imported from the Netherlands soon after bricks themselves came to England. Nevill, Curtis Green and Jekyll in *Old West Surrey* all illustrate the same elaborate example in Godalming High Street, which no doubt indicates the paucity of such work in Surrey. The main problem with this, and simpler examples of the same form, is the junction between the main roof and parapet. If it is not properly flashed there can he movement between the roof tiles and the brick gable which can mean leaks and rot to the main ridge joist.

House in High St., Godalming; Nevill

DORMERS

Curtis Green

Dormer windows, which are extremely common in all old buildings, only really differ from gables in their position and size; the structural solutions found in gables are repeated in dormers. The typical dormer is small with a single casement window lighting a room in the roof. However as we have seen at Betchworth (page 34) it is possible to build a very large dormer which can encompass a small room, though this is far from common and would tend to make for a very ungainly building.

Green illustrates a more typical dormer, with a timber frame filled with brickwork both angled and horizontal. The cheeks are rendered. Penty's detail is of a not dissimilar type, though here the gable is hipped, a very common form. The cheeks here are boarded, with flashing brought up behind the boarding; this joint is a very vulnerable one. Penty is being very traditional in his details here and certainly some of these would not be acceptable under today's bye-laws, which are on the whole wise when it comes to traditional building practice. He shows no overhanging cill at the bottom of the window and, it would seem, no flashing. Although it was rare in old buildings, a cill in this position is almost essential and it is also most important to flash with lead under it.

Where light is needed in the roof spaces of old buildings, it has, unfortunately, recently become common to break into them and fix patent roof lights. Many Planning Officers seem to prefer these to dormers, which are of course the correct way to light an attic. On very nearly every occasion roof lights are not satisfactory, either to the people using the rooms, which always seem cramped, but also and more importantly, to the look of the building from outside. Dormers, if properly designed, have an architectural quality that can enhance an old building. Whilst, as Planning Officers often suggest, roof lights may retain the roof line, they destroy the character of a roof by adding an alien hard shining element into the roof. Since a roof light is angled upwards it will always catch the light in quite a different manner than any other reflecting parts of the building. The windows of a dormer on the other hand, being vertical like all the other windows in the house, melt in with their surrounding.

The use of roof lights in the contentious areas of barn conversion is almost mandatory, since they are supposed to give a less domestic character to the converted barn. The barn at Mill Farm, Ockham with a great hipped dormer window in the roof, which since it is so well proportioned fits perfectly into the building, demonstrates that good fenestration need not detract from a barn's barn-ness.

Penty: Elements of Domestic Design

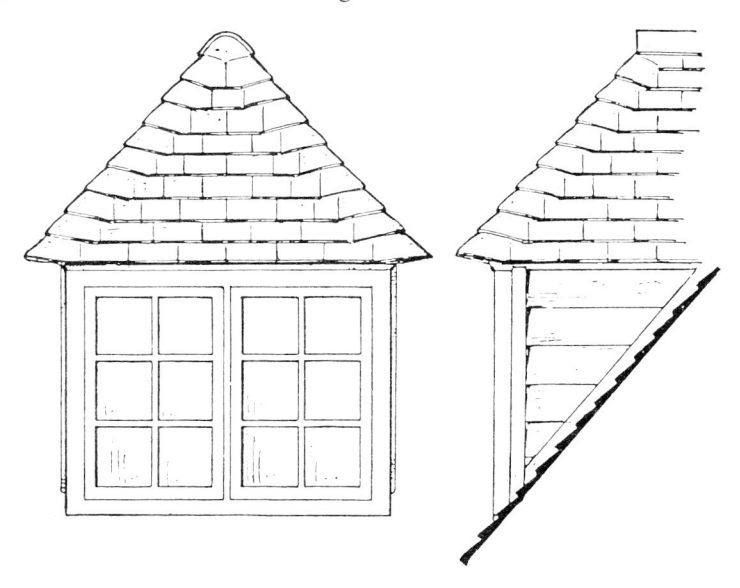

DETAILING: DORMERS

Mill Farm, Ockham in 1933. Surrey Local Studies Library

Eaves

The simplicity of the Surrey vernacular style is shown once again in the treatment of eaves. It is rare to find anything but the simplest of overhangs, which project just enough to keep any rainwater well away from the wall. Penty shows a number of details of these simple eaves. Figures 1 and 2 are the most commonly found on Surrey houses. The tiles lie on the rafters

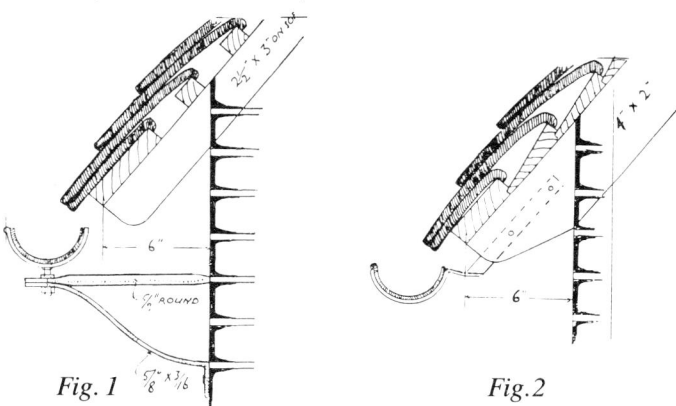

Fig. 1

Fig. 2

which project about six inches from the wall. It is normal for the gutter to be supported on a bracket from the wall.

Figure 3 shows examples of eaves with a brick corbel, which can sometimes give them a more finished look.

Fig. 3
Penty

HALF-TIMBERING

Originally Surrey, like so much of England, was heavily wooded and the the natural building material was timber framing with wattle infill. Today, though, it is rare to see half-timbered buildings in Surrey other than in one or two famous examples, like Great Tangley Manor. Most old buildings were in fact built of timber-framing but over the years they have been faced in brick, tile-hung or even plastered.

The Old Guest House, Lingfield, (now the County Library, described by Ian Nairn as "over-restored") is recorded in a series of early pictures (see following pages), which clearly show how so many Surrey houses have been treated over the years. When it was illustrated by Baily in his 1862 lecture, the 15th century Hall house had been divided into three cottages. Curtis Green draws details from the building and includes a photograph which from internal evidence, pre-dates the book, since it is not by Galsworthy Davie but by W.Page. A photograph dated August 1903 shows what Mr C. Foster Hayward had done in 1896-8.

The roof has been straightened and retiled, the end gable more elaborately tile-hung, many more timbers added to the end wall and the chimneys have been moved and completely redesigned, though still in a Surrey style. Green explains what happened. When Mr Hayward bought the house, "it had unfortunately been divided up, and for some time occupied, as three labourers cottages; all this was altered, and great care was taken by the late Mr Hayward to re-establish as much as possible of it in its original state." Although the house clearly needed repair we may feel today that Mr Hayward went a little too far in replacing structural elements that no longer existed.

Whatever the merits of the restoration, The Old Guest House at

DETAILING: HALF-TIMBERING

Lingfield is a fine example of a relatively unaltered Surrey half-timber building. Green's section, based on Hayward's perhaps rather fanciful re-creations, clearly shows the straightforward structural system used. On a stone base the main structural timbers, which held up the roof trusses, were built; between these there is a secondary series of vertical struts, and these bold cross purlins, the lower purlins raised above the stone plinth. Within these panels yet smaller uprights were fixed, and the spaces within were filled. At the beginning these would be filled with wattle and daub and would have but few windows, later the lower areas at least were filled with bricks. At the same time more window glass would have been added, though whether there would ever have been as much as Hayward suggests is doubtful. At the same time the tops of some of the windows might even have been given the rather elaborate Gothic arches shown here. The windows that Baily shows seem more likely to be original, both in shape and quantity.

Curtis Green: Shop at Lingfield

At the Old Guest House the upper rooms at either side of the front are corbelled out. Timber construction of course lends itself to corbelling, and Green gives a good example of how this is achieved in his details of a shop in Lingfield.

The gable at the Guest House seems always to have been tiled, (we can be sure that Mr Hayward would have displayed it had it not been so). Sometimes gables were intended to be seen, as at Bletchingly. Whilst the wall has been subjected to some somewhat eccentric alterations, the gable itself is a good example of a true half-timbered gable, where the final roof

THE SURREY STYLE

Bailly: "Remarks on Timber Houses" (top) W. Page in Curtis Green.

DETAILING: HALF-TIMBERING

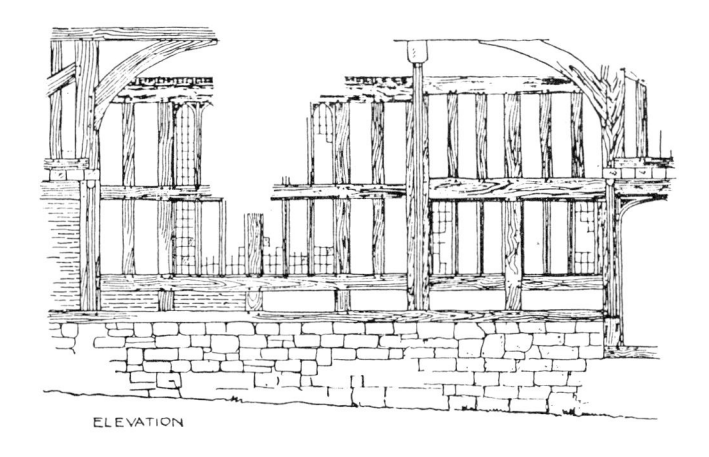

Curtis Green: section of wall, Guest House, Lingfield (below) In 1903, Surrey Local Studies Library

Curtis Green: Gable at Bletchingly; House at Bramley

truss, identical in outline to the internal trusses, displays itself on the exterior.

The straightforward and simple timber work on the Old Guest House is typical of most Surrey half-timbering. There are one or two buildings that are more elaborate, though there is nothing in Surrey to compare with even quite minor buildings in Shropshire. However there is one elaborate and rather artificial style that seems to have been popular with Surrey builders. This is the use of what Green calls curved braces, as at Bramley, and Great Tangley, which when they are placed side by side create the effect of rings of half timbering.

The belief that black timbers and white plasterwork is the correct finish for half-timber work dies hard. This is quite incorrect in Surrey. It was an invention of the early romantic movement, and was unfortunately given another lease of life by R.Norman Shaw. As early as 1888 Nevill was pointing out that this treatment was wrong. Curtis Green repeats: "The oak in these half-timber houses has usually weathered a most delightful silver-grey colour; the blackened timbers have been treated artificially and are hard and unpleasant in comparison with the natural colour." The same applies to the render infill, which should not be painted white but left in its more natural buff colour. In *Old West Surrey,* Jekyll records that the lime plaster coat was often mixed with ochre to give a softer colour next to the silvery greys of the wood.

TILE-HANGING

"In the habit of tile-hanging walls this county and its neighbour, Sussex, strike their most characteristic note. It is not, however, a practice of great antiquity, for Mr Ralph Nevill, who has given much study to the subject, is not inclined to date its introduction earlier than about 1700. The shapes of the tiles are many, but the most usual, except the simple oblong, is the rounded end. Where this weather tiling was used there was obviously a difficulty at the corner of walls. The ingenuity of later days adopted an angle tile, but originally it was the practice to stop the tiles against a corner post of oak". (Lawrence Weaver *Small Country Houses of Today I* 1910)

The main problem with half-timbering is that timber is not a material that readily stands up to damp weather. Sooner or later the ends will rot and finally the building will collapse. The obvious solution to this problem is to cover the timbers. This was normally done in two ways; either the whole building was faced in render or the walls were hung with tiles.

Rendered buildings must have been quite common in Surrey before the 19th century, Green shows an example in Galsworthy Davie's photograph of a farmhouse at Milford, an obviously half-timbered house that has been rendered. The majority of these buildings have now had their render stripped, whether the timber was intended to be displayed or not. The result is often to draw attention to bad mediaeval workmanship, giving an unfinished feeling to the building. This stripping of plaster, like the black painting of half-timberwork, is an unfortunate Victorian habit that is proving very difficult to eradicate. It is at the moment seen most prominently in the interior of churches and public houses, where, in a kind of Puritanical zeal, fine old plaster is all too often removed from interiors to display very mediocre stone or brickwork, leaving the interior both bleaker and less decorative than it was before.

Happily a tile-hung building does not seem to appeal to the strippers as plasterwork does, and so many fine examples of tile-hanging still survive in Surrey. Weather tiling, as it is often and appropriately called, belongs essentially to the Southern counties of England and the Netherlands - from whence it came. Originally it was an entirely practical solution to a structural problem. It was Norman Shaw who did much to popularise its use in modern buildings, in his weather tiled Surrey houses such as Merrist Wood, where in its tile-hung rear elevation Shaw comes nearest to the 'Surrey look' . Whilst the whole of the entrance front above the stone ground floor is overpoweringly half-timbered, the whole of the rear elevations are tile-hung in a rather unbending manner. The house is really too large, and these great areas of

House at Milford (Top). Shaw: Merrist Wood; Architecture II *(1897)*

tiling are too unbroken, for what in the end is more suitable for a small cottage than a mansion, which, whatever Shaw seems to be saying in his choice of materials, is what Merrist Wood really is. For tiles are much smaller than bricks, although they make a much more incisive pattern, and for this reason they do not look good over very large areas. This is something that the builders of the recent vernacular style buildings, who often use tiles in an attempt to make their large buildings seem humane, have yet to find out.

Black Hams Cottage; Surrey C.C.

On small buildings it is remarkable how much tile can be used. The Surrey County Council have a photograph, taken as late as 1970, which shows Black Hams Cottage at Elstead, which is entirely covered with tile work. It must be said that the result is not entirely satisfactory since there is little contrast between the wall tiles and the roof tiles. A rather more successful design was drawn by Nevill of a cottage at Chiddingfold. Here the tiling is brought right down to the top of the ground floor windows, and is carried up three stories into the gables. The result perhaps is still rather overpowering, but this cottage is interesting because it is clearly the source of

Nevill: Cottage at Chiddingfold

Lutyens' remarkable design of 1898 for Berrydowne House, over the Surrey border at Ash in Hampshire.

Another example of a heavily tile-hung house is Farm Place, Ockley. Here one elevation is almost completely tile-hung, whilst another front is half-timbered with only the corbelled-out gable tiled. The whole building seems to be in a ruinous state and it may well be that this is a case of tile-hanging being added to a decayed building in the perhaps idle hope that this would halt the decay.

At Ruckmans, Lutyens made brilliant use of tile-hanging to demarcate his additions to an old cottage. He makes a three storey addition which runs up to a triplet of gables, and these he completely hangs with tiles from immediately above the first floor windows. Notice the way that he handles his windows. Those on the second floor are wrapped round the ends of the walls, whereas the first floor windows stop just before the end of the gable. As well as giving lightness to what might otherwise be an overpowering display of weather tiling, the lower solid edges are functional, since there are columns at the rear which give strength to the wall where it is needed.

Most sucessful tile-hung Surrey cottages do not cover the wall surface

DETAILING: TILE-HANGING

Farm Place, (top); Surrey Local Studies Lib. Ruckmans, Country Life.

Nevill: Shop (bottom) and Cottage at Alfold
Falkner: detail of kick at foot of weather tiling; Farnham Museum

so thoroughly, the proportion of base wall to tile-hung wall is usually about equal. Examples of this can still be seen all over Surrey. Nevill draws numberless examples: three will suffice here, a cottage and a Drapers shop at Alfold, and the cottage at Dunsfold Common (see page 31). In all three the relationship between the base wall and the tile-hanging is about equal, and in all cases it is brought down to the top of the head of the ground floor windows and given a slight kick out to form a drip here. There is a detail of the 'kick' at the foot of tiled walls drawn by Harold Falkner, (kept with other of his drawings in the Farnham Museum). The tiling is taken over all the surfaces, whether the wall runs through in a straight line as at the cottage at Alfold, or whether there is a projection, as in the case of the shop and the cottage at Dunsfold. Both the Dunsfold and the Alfold cottages are gabled, and the tiling runs right up into the gables, though in the case of the Alfold cottage it is brought a little forward just after the gable starts, and the tiles may change character. This was quite a common practice, though not as common a practice as the Victorians later made it.

The whole matter of decorative tiles in buildings is contentious, there can be no doubt that they were used in old buildings, for instance in Linkfield Street, Redhill as photographed in 1887, but never in the flamboyant way that the Victorians used them, and indeed added them to old houses. See for instance the way in which Hayward treated the gable wall at the Old Guest House, Lingfield (page 102). As Green says; "neither on a roof nor on a wall, as weather tiling, do fancy shaped tiles, in my opinion, look so well as the straight... Perhaps the most satisfactory patterns are those produced by using straight-edged tiles of different colours in various forms of diaper. The tiles for this purpose were sometimes of the same make and colour when they left the potter's hands, the pattern developing only with age; one lot of the tiles forming the pattern had been dabbed with the bristles of a stiff brush before the tile was burnt, thus producing a rough surface which weathered more quickly than the ordinary hand-made tile."

Notwithstanding these remarks Green shows examples of a number of

Green

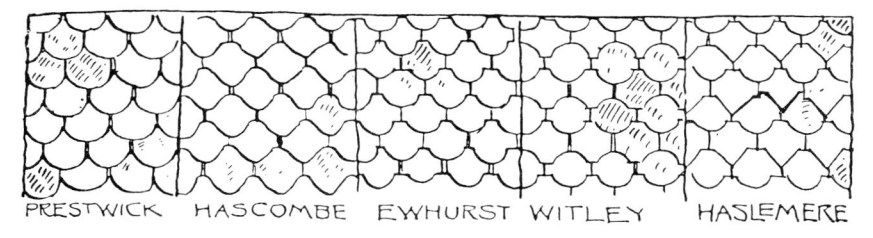

PRESTWICK   HASCOMBE   EWHURST   WITLEY   HASLEMERE

decorative tiles as does Nevill, who says of these, "pattern 'B' is that generally used. At Wonersh and Shere, and occasionally elsewhere, are examples of 'A', and I have fancied they had the appearance of being earlier in date than others. 'C' is, I think, only of modern date. At Haslemere are a great variety of patterns of weather-tiles, of which E, F. G, and H are examples not often found elsewhere, but 'E' is not uncommon over the Sussex border."

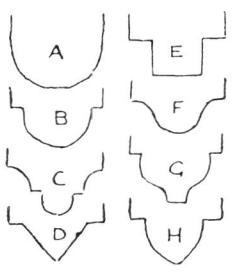

Nevill: tile shapes

Linkfield Street, Redhil; Surrey Local Studies Library

DETAILING: TILE-HANGING

The use of bands of decorative tiles in an old building can be seen at Valewood Farm, near Haslemere. Here, except for the lower tiles which curve out to form a drip, every other course has a decorative tile, similar to Nevill's pattern 'B' . This was the house in which that excellent architect Oliver Hill lived' in the years between the wars, and this picture shows Hill working in his garden. For this reason this picture should be looked at with some caution, for Hill was perfectly capable of 'improving' his cottage by adding these decorative tiles, and he was such a clever architect that he would be able to do this in a quite undetectable manner. Whilst the Surrey Local Studies Library has a number of examples of overall decorative tile patterning, such as the cottage at Ockley, taken before 1915, where most of the cottage is covered with half round tiles and the cottage at Witley in a photograph dated 1911, where sharply pointed tiles alternate with half rounds, there are no examples of decorative tiles in the bands that we see at Valewood. Most of the examples have quite straightforward tile-hanging in straight lines, like another, rather tumbledown cottage at Ockley photographed in 1890, or the straightforwardly neat tilework in the gable of a farmhouse at Ewhurst also photographed in 1890.

Valewood Farm; Titania Molyneux

THE SURREY STYLE

Cottage at Ockley; cottage at Witley; Surrey Local Studies Library

Gable at Ewhurst farm; cottage at Ockley; Surrey Local Studies Library

Cottage at Farley Green; (1915) Surrey Local Studies Library

Mention also must be made of the use of timber boarding to sheave the upper part of buildings. Boarding would of course have been cheaper than tiles but it doesn't survive as well, and so there are few extant examples of a material that must at one time have been very common in Surrey. The effect of the clapboarding is often neater than tile-hanging, note the way the corners have a small edging strip and the way that the bottom boards are kicked forward to make a drip, just as in tile work.

BRICK

Surrey is largely brick country and this is the building material that first comes to mind when we think of Surrey buildings. But surprisingly enough, in spite of the fact that they were used extensively by the Romans, there were few bricks in medieval Britain, and none in Surrey. The buildings of medieval Surrey would have been largely half- timbered with daub infill, as with the cottage described by Nevill as "near the station, Godalming." In just a few parts of the county it was possible to use stone but after the Merstham quarries ran out in the 16th century, no Surrey stone was of much quality.

Brick, being an expensive and modern commodity, was first used in the grand houses, of which the grandest, and one of the finest brick houses in England of its date, was Sutton Place near Guildford, built in the early 1520s. For smaller buildings it first came into use, as we have seen, as a fireproof material for chimneys. It was later used, because it was less susceptible to decay, as infill panels in half-timbering. Nevill has a drawing showing the way a panel is filled with Herring-bone brickwork. He points out that, "the notching shown on the face of the post in the illustration is generally found on the main posts, and, I believe, was made to receive the ends of supporting struts while the frame was being put up." He also suggests that "this mode of filling the panels is very unsuited to parts of a house exposed to the weather." Because of course there was no weather barrier between the brickwork and the timber.

It was soon realised that brick by itself laid as walls in front of the

DETAILING: BRICK

timber framing, made a very much better and more impervious wall at the ground floor at least. Above, the timber framing could be faced with the cheaper weather tiles. The Surrey Local Studies Library have a photograph of the inn in Chequers Lane, Walton-on-the-Hill being stripped before it was rebuilt in 1910, which clearly shows the rough timber frame, never intended to be seen, stripped of its tiles; below there is a well laid brick wall.

So the standard Surrey cottage look was born. It was not until quite late into the 19th century that we find brick used overall in cottages; the effect of this

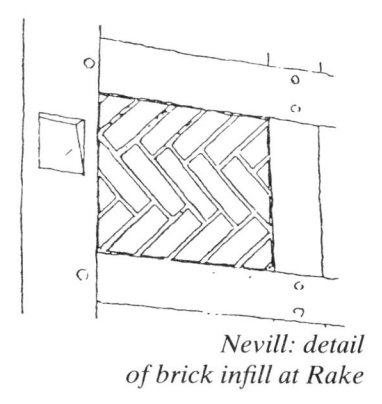

Nevill: detail of brick infill at Rake

Chequers Lane, Walton-on-the-Hill; (1908) Guildford Local Studies Library

great mass of unrelieved brickwork in The Beavers, at Farnham is somewhat overpowering. Earlier brick terraces, like the cottages at Bridge Square, Farnham are far less formidable, with their semi-circular arches over the windows and the first floor windows brought up tightly below the eaves formed of a simple dentilled brick design.

The Beavers, Farnham; R.C.H.M.E (Top) Bridge Square, Farnham

Nevill makes an important point about Surrey brickwork when in *The Builder* article of 1888 he talks of pointing; "the beauty of old brickwork", he says, "depends largely on these ½in. white joints. It is not only the small size of the bricks, but the large size of the joints, that gives the effect which it is so impossible for that reason to copy in modern work." Only a few years

DETAILING: BRICK

later he was to be proved wrong in that last sentence, for Lutyens and many others succeeded in getting brick makers to make thin bricks and bricklayers to lay them in thick mortar joints. This still applies today, it is perfectly possible to get authentic and sensitive brick laying if it is properly specified.

On more expensive buildings, such as the houses of Guildford and Godalming, we find by the 17th century all sorts of delightful patterned mannerist brick eccentricities. Nathaniel Lloyd in his *History of English Brickwork* of 1925, illustrates the survival of one wall of old Farnham Town Hall of 1674 in what Nairn calls; "a violent last fling of Artisan brickwork,

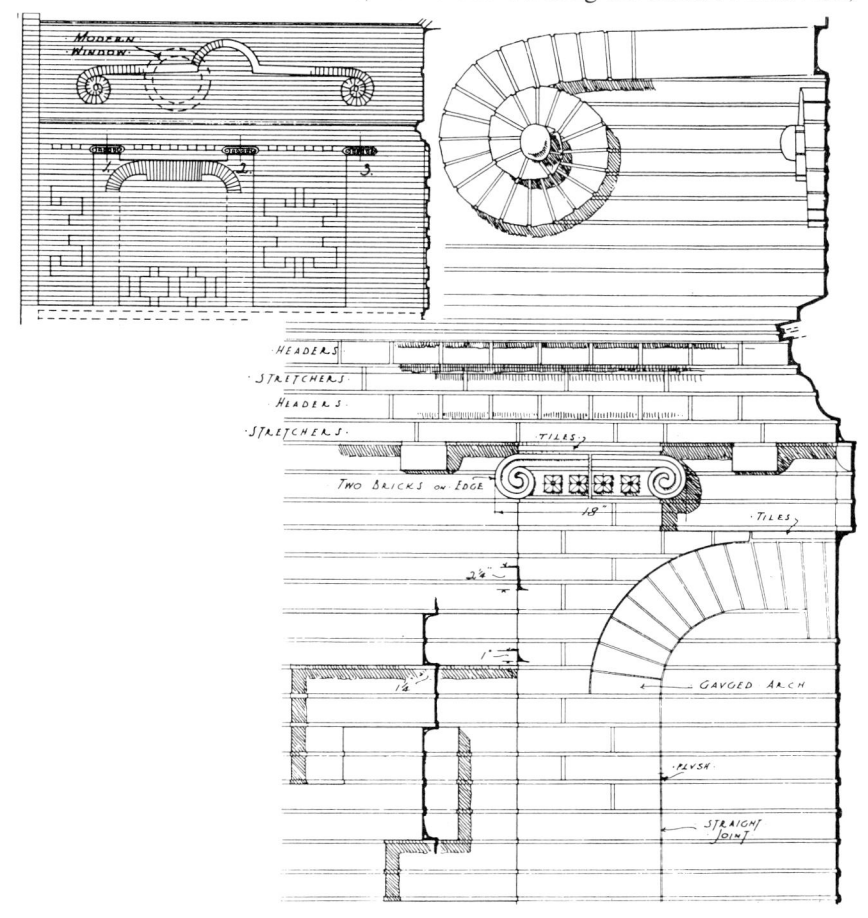

Nathaniel Lloyd: History of English Brickwork (1925) *Detail of Farnham Town Hall; 1; 2*

THE SURREY STYLE

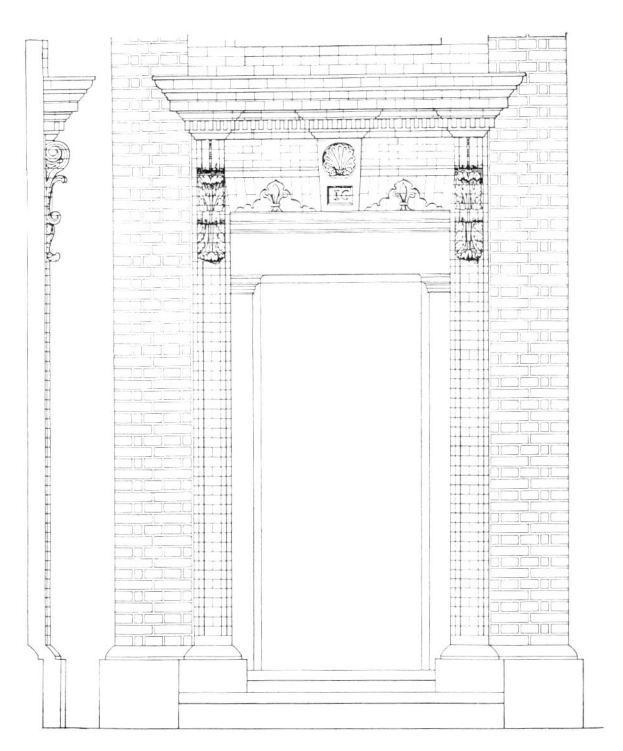

Lloyd: Detail of doorcase, Longbridge House.
Harold Falkner: Swimming pool entrance; Farnham Museum.

using the same jerky patterns as the houses in Godalming High Street." It was incorporated in the new town hall by Harold Falkner in the late 1930s. Figure 1 shows the two fragments that have survived, and Figure 2 gives a detail of the wildly inaccurate classical architecture. Every capital is slightly different, and in one case a pair of pilasters are joined by an arch which crashes in below the columns, whereas another pair have a soldier arch acting in the same manner. Lloyd next illustrates the doorcase to what he calls The Convent, (in fact Longbridge House, 3 Downing Street,) Farnham, dated 1717, the change in just over forty years could not be more remarkable. Here the carefully cut and rubbed bricks conform exactly to the most correct classical principles, the brickwork exactly copying timber doorcases in contemporary London houses. By 1717 in fact the rich little Surrey towns, already almost suburban, were no longer in any sense provincial, but even as far out as Farnham, part of 'the great wen'. And so London standards of bricklaying apply; notice that the bricks of Longbridge House are laid in a complex Flemish bond, whereas most simple Surrey houses were laid in the more normal English bond.

The earlier elaborate cut and ribbed brickwork was taken up by the Victorian architects of Surrey, in particular Norman Shaw and Lutyens' master, Ernest George. But the next generation eschewed such excitements and rarely used elaborate brickwork, though Harold Falkner nearly always used brick in his buildings, for Farnham more than any other in Surrey is a brick town. In the Farnham swimming pool entrance, built as a memorial to Queen Victoria's Jubilee of 1897, we find Falkner using very narrow rubbed bricks to form his rustications and voussoirs. As we have seen at Tancreds Ford (see Plate 12) Falkner used clever brick rustication on many of his houses, in a style that was not particularly typical of Surrey and probably ultimately derives from Basil Champney's Newnham College at Cambridge. But it was used after Falkner by so many architects building in Surrey, that this type of detailing has become the adopted Surrey style.

STONE

Whilst brick is almost universally used in Surrey, stone is localised to the small area around Godalming served by the Bargate quarries. To quote the introduction to The Buildings of England - *Surrey:* "in Bagshot Sands there are occasional deposits of dark brown gravelly conglomerate or carstone looking like nutty toffee - and also boulders of grey-green heathstone, scattered about the landscape... It gives a mellow individual texture -. The principle Surrey building stone, called Mersham or Reigate stone, came from the very narrow beds of the Upper Greensand immediately south of the chalk escarpment. It is greenish-grey, mellow, easily worked and unfortunately easily eroded... It was sufficiently highly thought of for the quarries, which were Crown Land, to be restricted in the 12th and 13th centuries to royal or ecclesiastical use... In the Lower Green sand several beds have been worked, some dark brown (mainly around Oxted and near Farnham), more often greenish-grey and greenish-brown, quarried around Godalming and known as Burgate (sic) stone. This was almost always used as rubble, not ashlar, giving cottages in villages like Thursley or Hascombe their typical soft outline, often made softer still by galletting, or sticking tiny chips of stone into the courses of mortar."

In fact this use of Bargate stone in cottages is really quite rare, Green illustrates a single example; Nevill only gives two not very enlightening drawings of cottages at Binscombe, which he says, "are partly built of rough Bargate stone with brick dressings. The wide joints of the rough stone are stuck over with small black ironstone pebbles, called 'galleting'. "Interestingly he then goes on to say, "This is distinctly a Jacobean feature, and I think not to be found in older work." Gertrude Jekyll in *Old West Surrey* gives a detail of galleting between the joints of a Bargate stone wall, with typical brick edging. Of it she says: "local custom decorates the rather wide or uneven mortar joint with small pieces of the black ironstone. The bricklayers (sic) call it garoting or garneting; there seems to be no general agreement as to the exact word." Today galleting seems to be the agreed term for this custom.

If it was little used in old cottages, Bargate stone was certainly used a great deal by the arts and crafts architects, we have already seen Thackeray Turner using it in his own house, Westbrook, Godalming (pages 55–9). Another important Arts and Crafts architect was Alfred Powell and on the ridge south of Pitch Hill, Hurtwood Common he built a house called Long Copse, immediately next door to and sharing the same views as Philip Webb's Coneyhurst and next to the site of what was to become in the 1920s Oliver Hill's Marylands. Whilst Webb's

Detail of galleted wall;
Old West Surrey

red brick house is a little dull and Hill's house, with its green pantiles, is frankly exotic, Powell makes every effort to make his rich woman's weekend house look like a simple country cottage.

The house was originally built in 1897 as a two roomed summer cottage for a Mrs Mudie-Cooke and Powell acted as Master of the Works. According to Lawrence Weaver in *Small Country Houses of Today:* "He bought all materials, and the craftsmen (save the plumbers - an entertaining exception) were University men who worked with him. - The result is instinct with simplicity while free from affectation."

We may take the work of the University men with a pinch of salt for there is nothing amateurish in the craftsmanship at Long Copse. The coursing of the faced rubble Bargate stone is very fine, as are the flush dressed stone mullions to the windows. These mullions are a very sensible solution to the problem of Bargate stone, which does not lend itself to any form of elaborate carving. The way in which Powell brings his leaded metal windows right up to the face of the building has good vernacular precedent. It does also have an aesthetic quality, beautifully brought out in André Goulancourt's brilliant photograph, where the evening sun catches the glass of windows, which being on exactly the same plane as the wall, gives an

André Goulancourt: two views of Long Copse

amazing solidity to the building.

The cottage was originally built with four rooms under the thatch roof, however Mrs Mudie-Cooke soon decided to make it a more permanent home and so a kitchen wing was added at right angles, and to emphasise the accretive quality this new wing was roofed in large Horsham stone tiles. Later a further outhouse was built on to the kitchen and the roof continued down at a slightly flatter pitch in the manner that we have seen on countless early cottages. The thatched cottage at the rear was built for the staff, for in Edwardian times the simple life was never that simple.

Long Copse is a straightforward solution to building a simple living place which still fits into its surroundings, and is the type of cottage that could easily be built today, using ordinary country building techniques. Except that perhaps the cost of stone might present some problems, there is no reason why this should cost more than most modern houses. The only thing missing today is the willingness of designers and builders to subordinate their ego to the needs of the site. In East Anglia Stephen Mattick has recently built such cottages, but so far no such architect builder has appeared in Surrey. It will probably not be long now before something similar is tried in the county.

DETAILING: STONE

Lutyens also used Bargate stone in nearly all his important Surrey buildings. In Munstead Wood and The Orchards the rubble stonework is laid without any additional features, as it is in the house at Fulbrook. But in the separate stables the walls are built with coursed Bargate rubble and the enormous chimneys are in a contrasting bright red brick. In contrast there is a line of red tiles which form a lintel to the oak windows. In the gable Lutyens has formed a jokey pediment in tiles over the window. But his most extreme piece of fun comes in a tiny window in the great chimney breast. This is given an enormous voussoir made up of tiles on edge and slivers of stone. There seems to be little precedent in all Surrey for this escapade.

Detail of wall, Fulbrook Stables; Surrey C.C.

This little Fulbrook building of 1897 should give us a warning of what was to come only two years later at Tigbourne Court. This famous design is a riot of tile decorations in sober, but galleted Bargate stonework. On the famous entrance front, there are no more than eleven courses of stone before there runs a decorative line of tiles, and these tiles are not flat but formed into a herring bone pattern (Plate 14). On the first floor windows of the main facade Lutyens has played the same trick with a tiled pediment as he did at Fulbrook, though this time he is much more sophisticated. Here the pediments to the brick mullioned windows alternate between round and

THE SURREY STYLE

sharp in a frankly Mannerist way. Down below there are paired classical columns in an irregular spacing. The whole elevation reminds one of the show front of a Jacobean house, could this be a reflection of Nevill's views on galleting?

Round the corner in the garden there is another delightful detail, a balcony to the main bedroom. (Plate 15) Here, in the way Lutyens combines brickwork, including a great curving brick corbel with the galleted stonework, he displays his complete mastery of traditional Surrey building forms. It shows how a great artist can take the simplest of building materials and bring them together to form them into a romantic yet almost perfect composition.

DOORS

Like most of the details that we have so far been considering, the actual structural elements in cottage doors are very simple, and continued to be

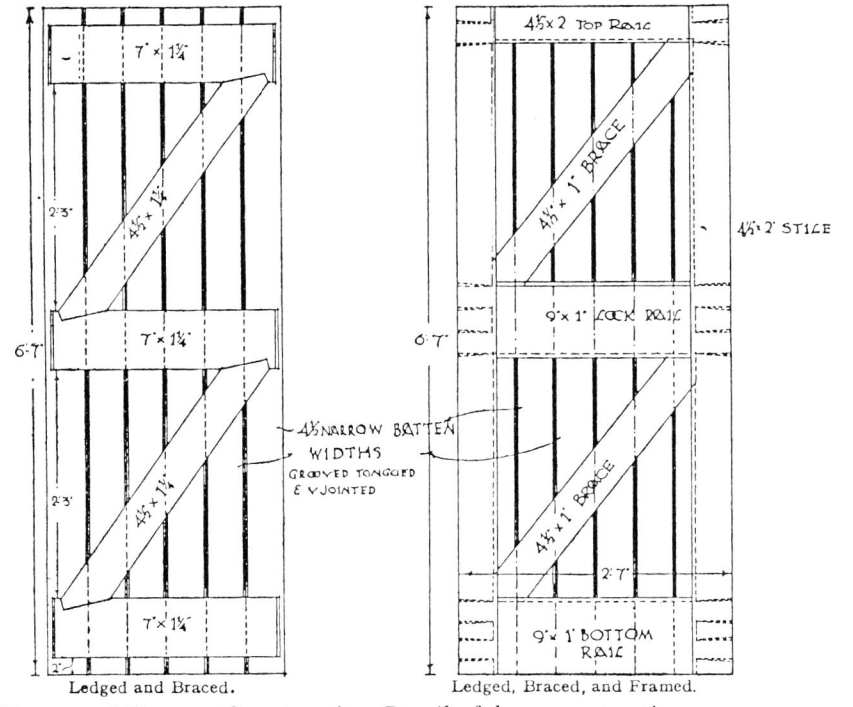

House and Cottage Construction *Detail of door construction*

made in much the same fashion until the time of the mass produced flush door. We take our detail from an ordinary builders' text book, *House and Cottage Construction*, published between the wars. The normal cottage door would be ledged and braced as shown in the Figure 1, with wide ledges, often considerably wider than the seven inches shown here, and narrower braces, here shown at four and a half inches. A superior door might be framed on the outer edges, as shown in Figure 2. In either case they would be faced on the outside with vertical battens, which would always be tounged and grooved and frequently V jointed to give a show face.

The interest in these doors is not their construction but the opportunity that they gave of moulding the face timbers. The ledges and braces might be moulded on their edges, to give a finer interior finish; this became a favourite detail of Lutyens and other arts and crafts architects like Detmar Blow. The exterior battens, which could be of any practical width, however, give an opportunity for more interesting mouldings. Green draws a number of examples of these doors. The door at Newdigate has merely three boards in a width of two foot nine inches. The reason why it is so heavily nailed is that in this case these vertical boards are a facing to horizontal cross boarding. This is to make the door more secure and weather proof. The diagonals at the bottoms show where the door has been repaired. This part on an exterior door is a place vulnerable to rot particularly in exposed positions, since the rain tends to collect here. However this can be easily overcome by a weather bar fixed at an angle at the bottom of the door. Although not so common on old doors as it is today it is a practical and not unsightly solution to a serious problem.

The door from the Abbot's Hospital, Guildford has four boards, but these have been simply V moulded. The most elaborate of these doors that Green shows is from Puttenden, The panels here have each had six V grooves cut into them.

All Green's examples' have relatively simple mouldings, but Nevill shows some more complex mouldings. Example A with its double sided diamond cut comes from Hawlands and B which combines a diamond with a small ovolo moulding shows how complex some of the boarding to these doors can be. Probably these two doors were intended for internal use. Example C is much more functional and comes from Godalming. Here simple cover strips are fixed over the joints of the battens. This is precisely the detail that Lutyens used to his garden door at Munstead Wood. There is no reason why all the doors shown here should not be reproduced, they would all be considerably cheaper than the fielded panelled doors that are regularly made in most good joiner's shops, which, however well made, are not suitable for cottages.

THE SURREY STYLE

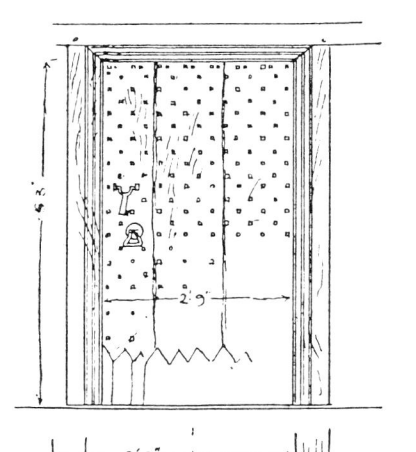

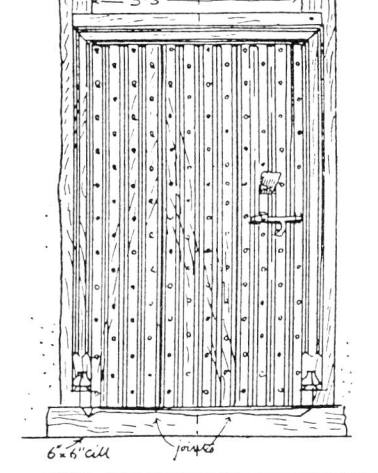

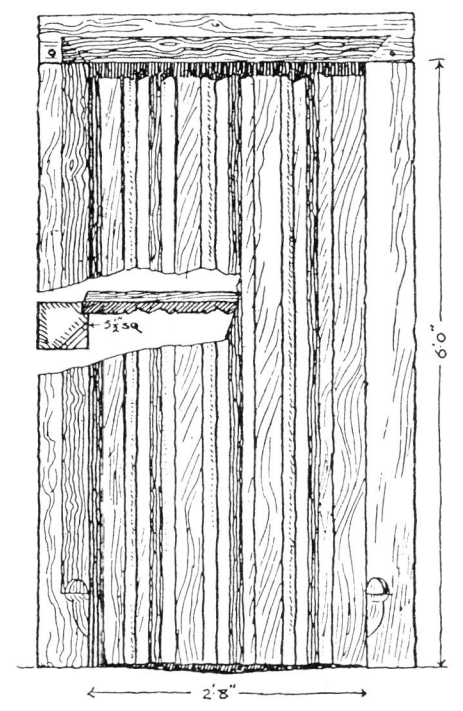

Green: doors from (1) Newdigate (2) The Abbot's Hospital, Guildford (3) Puttenden Nevill: sections of doors Detail of door, Munstead Wood; André Goulancourt

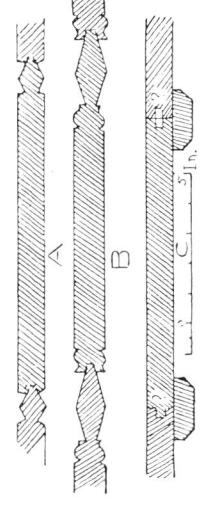

DETAILING: DOORS

As can be seen from Munstead and Green's detail of the Abbot's Hospital, the frames to these doors both inside and out were very simple but massive. Green's frame is a five and a half inch square of oak, with a simple chamfer and a very small rebate for the door. Though the frames can be very much reduced from this size they must still have some body since architraves should never be used on these types of doors.

The shape of the doors that Green shows are different to the shape that we are used to today where the standard size is two foot six inches by six foot three. The Guildford door is two foot eight inches wide by six foot high. This door would of course be too low today, and if the height were increased to

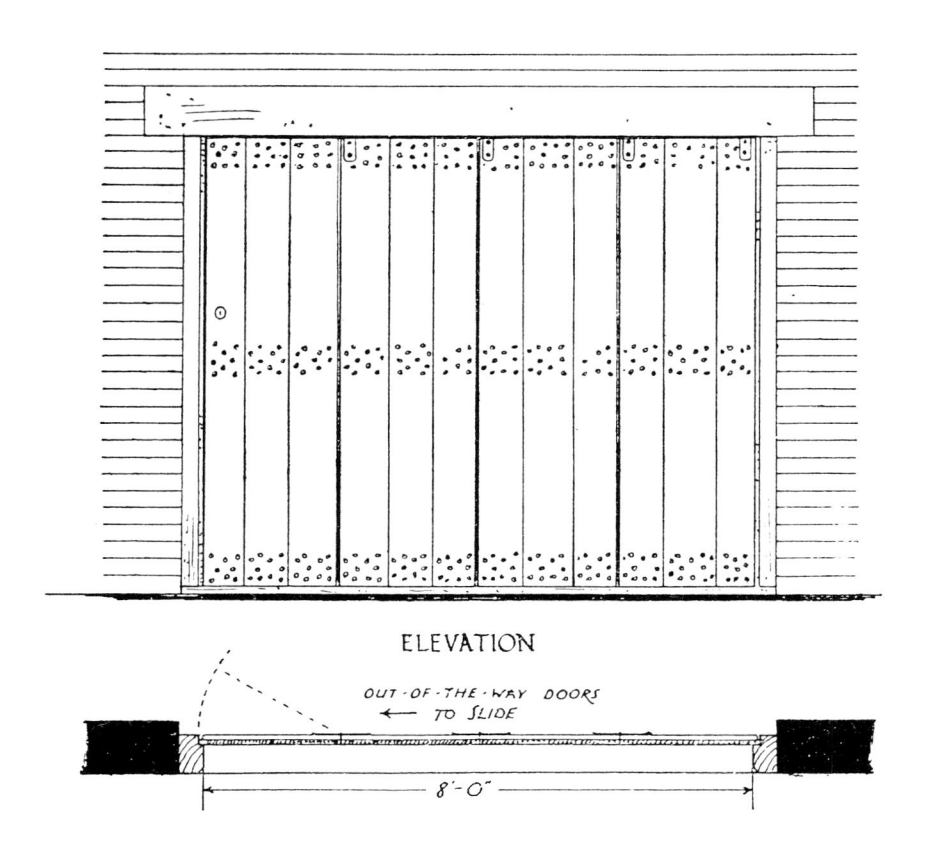

ELEVATION

OUT-OF-THE-WAY DOORS
← TO SLIDE

8'-0"

Penty: Elements of Domestic Design

a more normal six foot three inches then the width, increased relatively, would be nearly two foot eleven inches wide, and this gives a very much more satisfactory shape and size to a front door. The arts and crafts architects in fact made their front doors much wider than this, there are a number of doors by Detmar Blow well over three foot six inches wide, though their heads are no higher than average.

Whilst front doors may have been wider, there was of course no precedent in an old building for doors for double garages. Penty came up with rather a satisfactory design for these. He shows a four leaf sliding folding door; the number of leaves could of course be increased, each leaf here is two foot wide formed of three vertical battens. "The top and bottom ledges being at the edges;" Penty remarks, "no bead or V-joint is put at the edge of the battens, as in my opinion they are better omitted. The battens should be fastened to the ledges with hurdle nails, which give the same appearance as the old fashioned smith-made nails. The rows of these nails relieve the monotony which otherwise a batten door inevitably has."

WINDOWS

Whilst doors present few difficulties to anyone proposing to repeat traditional details, it is a different matter with windows. In the years immediately after 1920 the Building Research Station gave a hard look at many traditional building details and their findings are reflected in the requirements of the Building Bye-laws. The bye-laws are a straightforward response to practical problems, in particular the problems of rainwater and heat loss. Traditionally cottage windows in Surrey have always been fixed on the face of the building, and we have seen how visually satisfactory this can be in Alfred Powell's delightful Long Copse at Hurtwood (see page 123). As another important arts and crafts house builder E.Guy Dawber remarked in *The Studio Year Book 1908,* windows "should be treated as organic parts of the wall and not mere openings surrounded by stone-work. Windows should always give a sense of enclosing, or of separation from the outside".

However the bye-laws call for windows to be brought well inside the face of the wall, usually something like four inches, so that a good drip can be formed at the head, to prevent rain running down the face of the window and getting in. At the same time there must be a timber cill, which projects from the face of the window with a groove under to form a drip, and this should preferably project over a stone, tile or concrete cill. Any horizontal mullions should also project forward of the windows to form a drip, and preferably the opening windows themselves should be rebated and proud of the frame. If such windows are fitted - and of course all standard windows follow this practice - this can considerably change the character of an old building, and so should be avoided. Other means have to be found to make windows weather tight.

Penty, writing in the late 1920s, was already aware of these problems and he published a number of details for windows fixed almost flush to the face of the wall which go a certain way to solving this problem. Figure 1 shows leaded lights fixed into a simple painted deal frame; here only the timber cill, which has a drip, projects. The only other defence against water penetration is at the jamb, where there is a small amount of render to the brickwork and a throated water barrier. Figure 2 show details of oak windows, Figure 3 giving large scale details of the windows shown on fig. 2. Although these are shown in oak they look just as well in painted softwood, though Penty rightly says that the size of the timbers should be reduced if paint is used since otherwise the painted frames tend to become too conspicuous. Oak is not a wood that much lends itself to elaborate mouldings and the mullions are almost completely plain, only the transome is throated. Once again the frames are brought right to the front of the building, and alas much of the Penty detailing would be unacceptable today. Whilst the jamb and the cill has a water check, the most vulnerable place, the head, has neither a drip nor a check. Nonetheless this is the type of detail that has usually proved to be entirely satisfactory in buildings for centuries. As Penty says; "many architects imagine that in order to keep out the weather it is necessary to make the transome project and to throat it on the underside. But the arrangement is both ugly and unnecessary. I have used this section for over twenty years and have not had a single complaint; what happens is that the water gets no further than the cavity. It runs down the side of the sash and discharges itself at the sill." Penty does not explain what would happen if the cavity were to get blocked. It may well be that we are today liable to over-detail against weather penetration, though with professional liability as it is today it is a foolish architect who ignores the instructions of the framers of the building bye-laws.

Penty's leaded lights are bedded directly into the timber frames and the opening lights are formed with standard metal windows' opening light sections, fixed into similar rebate as the fixed lights. It is essential that the glass here lines through as nearly as possible with the fixed panes. When this is done properly the result can be very satisfactory, as can be seen in a 1911 advertisement for Hope's metal windows.

Oddly enough it was common from quite early times to use metal - wrot iron - opening lights set in wooden frames, which is not common today. Nowadays, in contrast to the 1930s, builders rarely use standard metal

THE SURREY STYLE

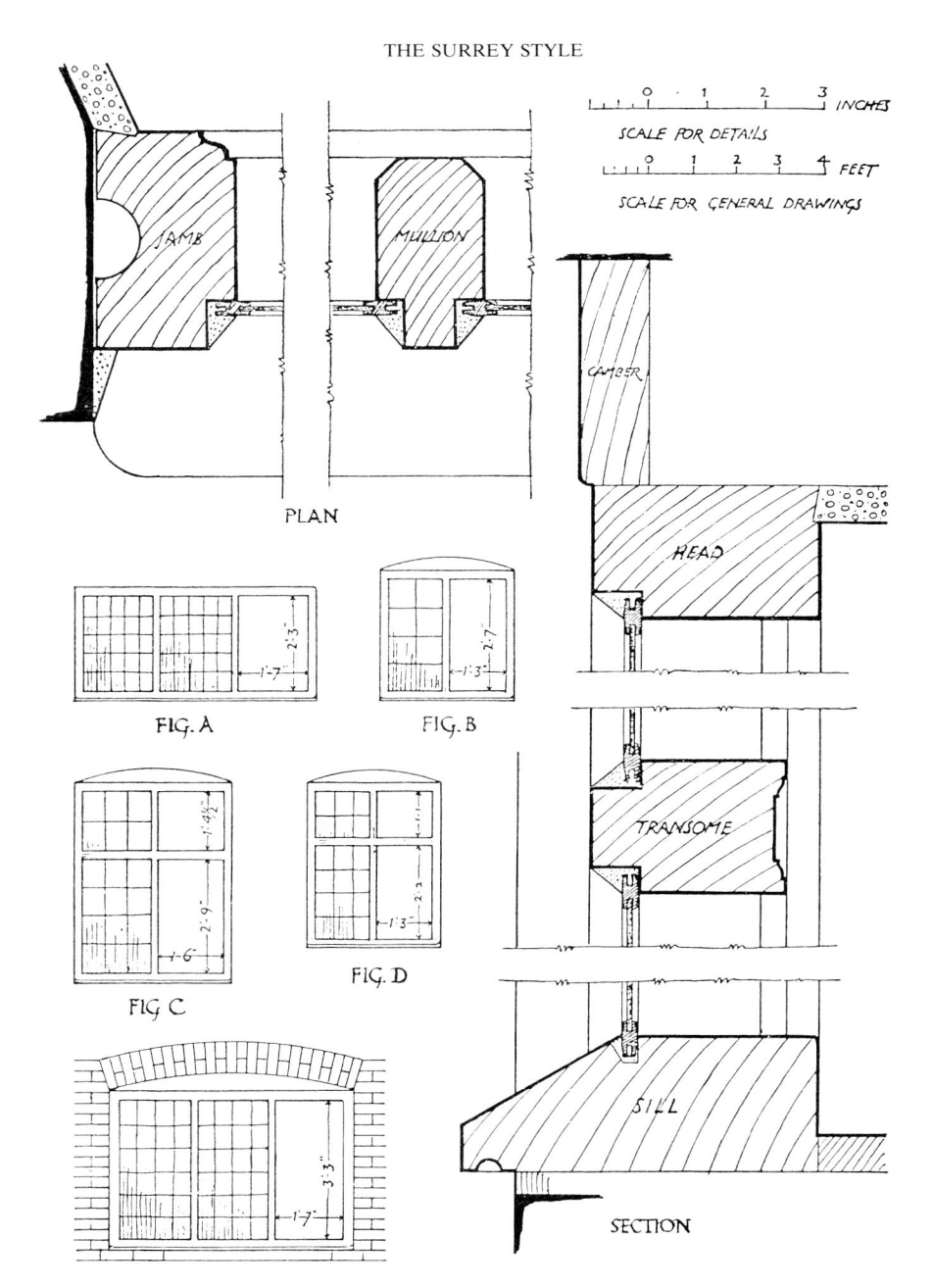

Penty: Elements of Domestic Design *(1)*

DETAILING: WINDOWS

EXTERNAL ELEVATION

INTERNAL ELEVATION

SCALE OF FEET

PLAN

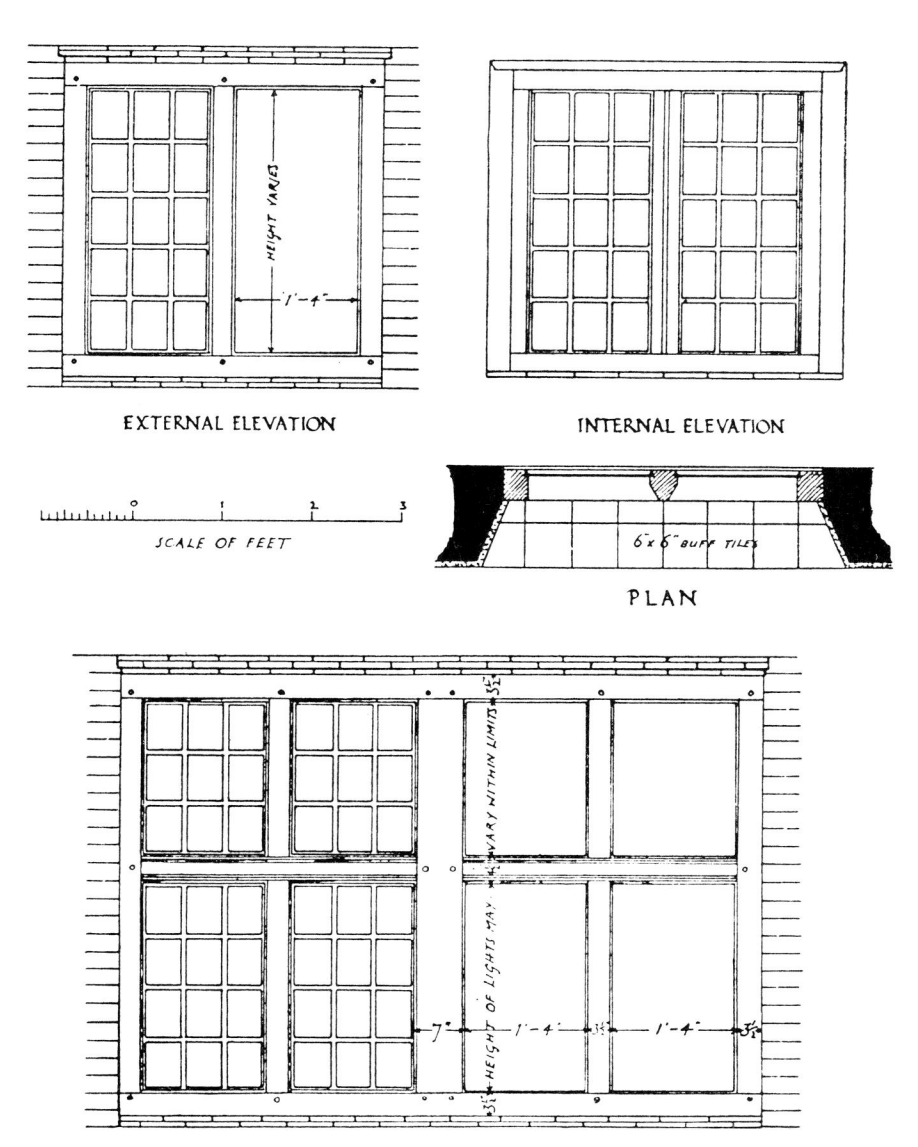

FOUR LIGHT WINDOW WITH TRANSOME AND DOUBLE MULLION

Penty: Elements of Domestic Design *(2)*

THE SURREY STYLE

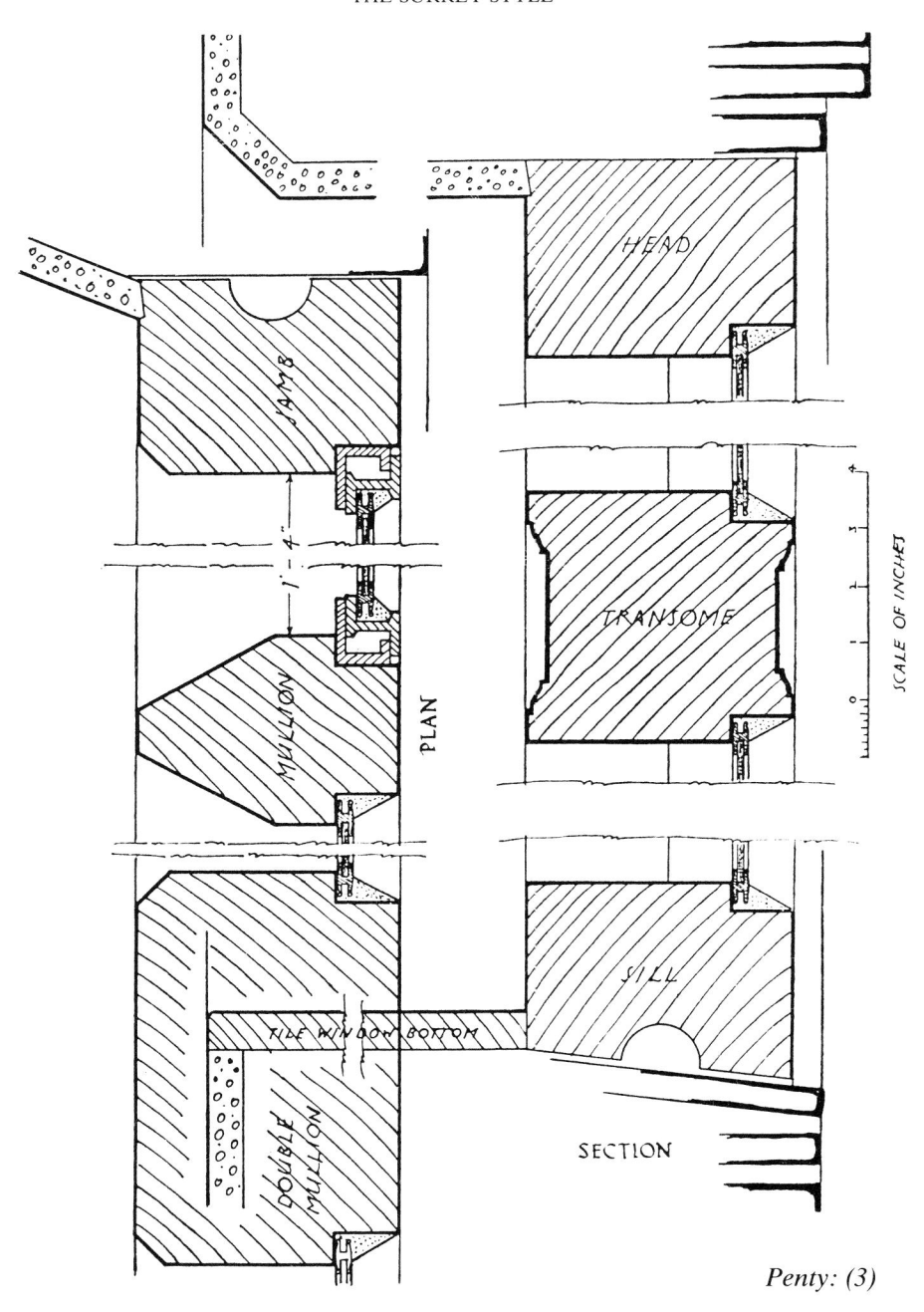

Penty: (3)

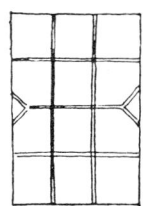

Hope's Metal Windows, 1911. Green: Glazing at Oxted.

windows preferring mass produced wooden windows. Though they are without a doubt more weather proof than the older windows, and can be double glazed, the way in which all the opening lights project from the frames leads to a far less satisfactory visual effect, losing all the organic quality that Dawber admired.

Penty also deals with the layout of leading in cottage windows, and Figure 1 shows windows, which he says are drawn at random from cottages and farmhouses in the Chilterns, which differ little from Surrey examples. "It will be seen," he says, "that the variation in the individual lights and their subdivision into leaded light panes is enormous. Yet they look alright." From these drawings it is obvious that there is considerable leeway in the number of panes that can be used. Penty shows a number of panes from five across to only two, but probably the most satisfactory is Figure C, a window with three panes across, and four down. Obviously the number of panes is affected by the size of the window, and on all occasions the panes must be a true upright rectangle. Although diagonal leaded lights were quite common in old buildings they were never used by the arts and crafts architects. Diamond leading never gives the impression of being authentic, no doubt because it still smacks of the suburban bungalow or the cottage orné. The new practice of planting lead strips on to plain sheets of glass is of course quite unsatisfactory. Not only are the lead strips impermanent, but visually it has none of the quality of genuine leading, for in a genuine leaded window each pane of glass is set at a slightly different angle, which gives a slight rippling reflection.

Both Nevill's drawings and the photographs in the Surrey archive show that the majority of old cottages, in Surrey had leaded lights. Timber glazing bars in cottages are a relatively new invention, though when they are simply detailed as ordinary casements, preferably without top hung ventilators, they can look perfectly decent. Standard casement windows are rarely satisfactory since they are made to metric dimensions (dimensions quite foreign to all old buildings) and, as we have seen, the way in which the opening lights are planted on the outside of the frame does not give a homogeneous effect. The recent habit of staining, rather than painting, exterior timber should be avoided at all costs, the reliability of the varnish stain over long periods has yet to be put to the test, but more importantly stained timber does not sit happily with brickwork, where it is too close a match, or stone where it contrasts harshly. Normally ordinary timber windows should be painted white, with the metal parts black, and oak should be waxed and allowed to develop into a natural silver colour.

DOOR FURNITURE, IRONMONGERY AND CRAFTSMANSHIP

Green: detail of window furniture

Metal door latches and bolts were common enough on cottage doors; Green's drawing of the door on Newdigate shows one (p. 128). Wooden latches were also common, and Green in his drawing of the door at Puttenden (p. 128) shows such a latch, presumably on an outside door, but this was more commonly an internal detail. Penty gives a detail of a wooden latch in his book (opposite). This is a straightforward affair, the 'lock' is a mere wedge - which is a very effective way of locking a door. It is a design which can easily be reproduced by a good joiner today. It should be made of the same wood as the door, though it is not practical to paint it. The result will be more homogeneous and it will certainly give a more authentic look than a modern mass produced metal latch or even a so called hand-wrot-iron latch.

Of course all window ironmongery must be made of metal but on the whole wrot iron should be avoided in ironmongery. There are few iron smiths today capable of reproducing old work without changing the proportions or adding unnecessary tool marks, which is odd because this is one of the few old building crafts that has survived as a genuine hand craft.

PLAN OF WEDGE

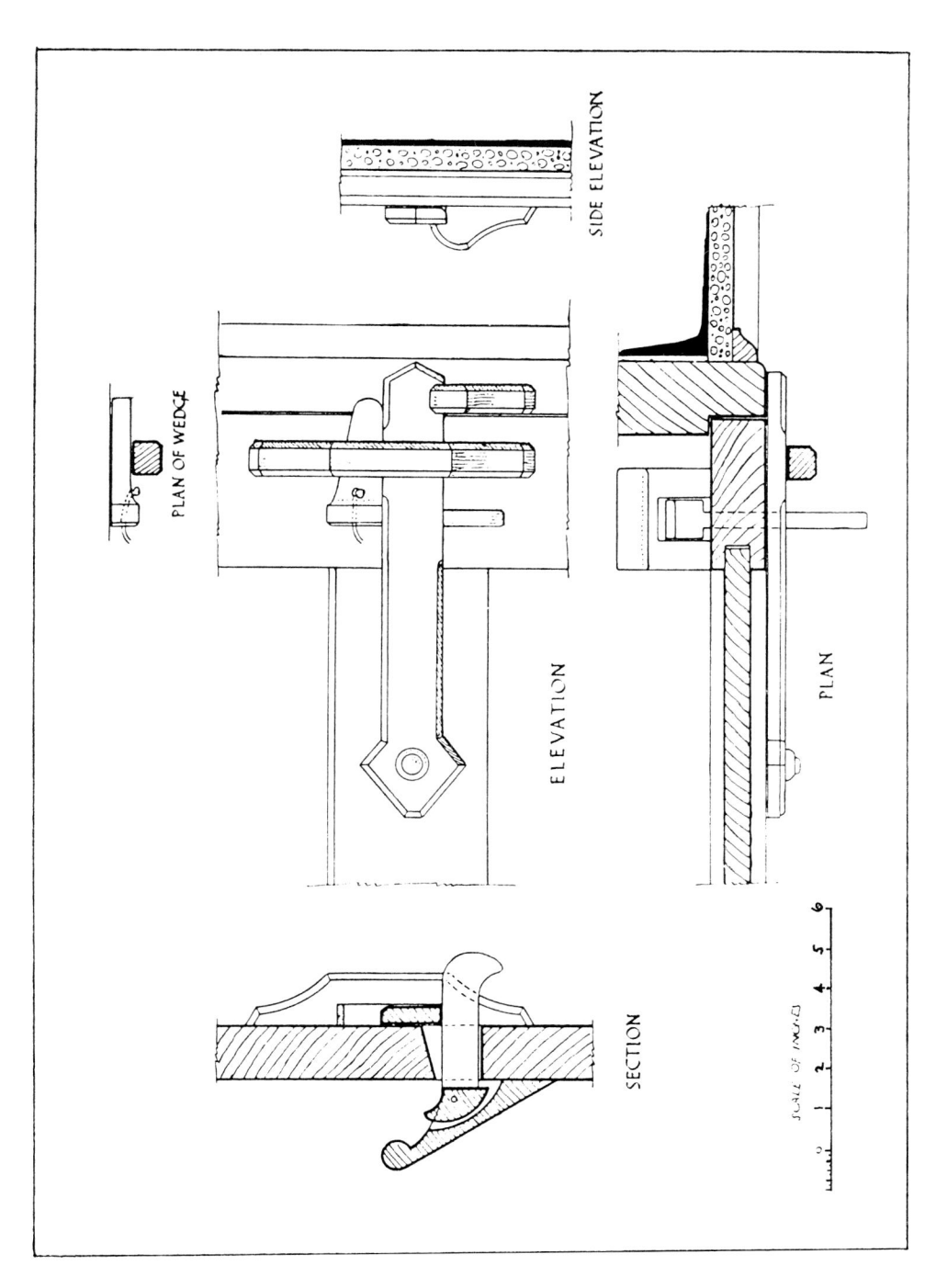

SIDE ELEVATION

ELEVATION

PLAN

SECTION

SCALE OF INCHES

Green shows a number of details of old metal work, but it would be hard to find a smith today capable of copying them without his seeing to it that every blow of the hammer is made to read. This may be good for his own self regard but it does nothing for the wrot iron.

The reason of course why smiths go in for this exaggerated hand-crafted look is that it is demanded by the purchaser who must have something to show for his extra expense. It is almost always the fault of the customer, and very often the architect also, if old buildings are shoddily treated; after all the builder is unfortunately only there to do what he is told.

This is hardly the place to discuss the whole matter of building craftsmanship today. But I have found that in normal day-to-day building where the craftsman is set to go about his traditional trade, such as roofing, bricklaying and joinery, there is nothing to worry about. It is only plastering which presents problems. Plaster itself and the techniques of plastering have changed considerably since the 1930s, and it is now almost impossible, using modern equipment, to reproduce the slight bumps and imperfections that gave old plasterwork so much of its character. As well as this the plasterer has learnt, over a long period now, how to create an entirely smooth surface, and on most work this is an entirely appropriate finish. It is wrong to ask a craftsman, like an iron smith or a plasterer, to give spurious character to his work. The detestable swooping lumps of plaster that one see on the walls of too many pubs are the result of this; if old plasterwork is to be reproduced something much subtler than this must be done, and this can only be done by discussion with the craftsman whilst looking at old work.

THE POSSIBILITY OF RECREATING OLD WORK TODAY

If this book has had any purpose it is to show that it is perfectly possible to retain the quality and character of old buildings, both in extensions and in newly built houses. New houses can of course be quite as destructive to old Surrey towns or the Surrey landscape as any insensitive addition. I have tried to show from the work of that great chain of late 19th century architects, craftsmen and clients (and the client is one of the most important links in that chain) how to build in the spirit of the old builders and in this way to preserve both the buildings and the countryside around them for future generations.

That greatest of all Surrey clients, Gertrude Jekyll, working with the greatest of Surrey architects, Edwin Lutyens, encapsulates that quality when writing in 1901 of her then newly built house, Munstead Wood. "Does it often happen to people who have been in a new house only a year and a half, to feel as if they had never lived anywhere else?"

ACKNOWLEDGEMENTS

The generosity and assistance of the following individuals and institutions have made this book possible:

The Illustrations:
John Janaway, Senior Librarian
The Surrey Local Studies Library, Guildford

André Goulancourt

Dr Nigel Barker; County Planning Department, Surrey County Council, Kingston upon Thames

Marley plc

Mr and Mrs David Graham, Hon. Secretaries
Mrs Janette White, Assistant Librarian,
Surrey Archaeological Society, Guildford

Stephen Croad; Royal Commission on the Historical Monuments of England

Anne Jones, Curator, Wilmer House, Farnham

Sam Lloyd for permission to reproduce his Grandfather, Curtis Green's drawings

Alan Powers

The Architectural Association

Francis Graham did the picture research

The Text:
Bridget Rees; David Coombs

INDEX OF ARCHITECTS

Baillie-Scott, M.H. 8, 14, 48, 49
Baily, Charles 11–12, 37
Baker, Herbert 10
Blomfield, Reginald 10
Blow, Detmar 130
Caroë, W.D. 33, 48–50, 60
Champneys, Basil 121
Cornell Ward and Lucas 18
Dawber, Guy 10, 130, 135
Falkner, Harold 8, 10, 36, 65 67–9, 111, 121
George, Ernest 55, 121
Green, W. Curtis *passim*, 13, 23, 32
Hayward, C. Foster 100–1
Hill, Oliver 113, 123
Jack, George 41
Jekyll, Gertrude 8–10, 41, 83
Lethaby, R. 10
Lorimer, W.R. 10
Lutyens, Edwin 8–10, 14, 15, 23, 32, 33, 36, 41, 45–8, 49, 51, 53, 56, 59–64, 65–7, 70–2, 78, 79, 80, 88, 91, 92, 108, 119, 125, 126, 127, 138
Mattick, Stephen 124
May, E.J. 4, 75, 88–9
Nevill, Ralph *passim*, 7, 8, 12–14, 16, 43–5, 51, 76, 79
Newton, Ernest 8
Niven and Wigglesworth 10
Penty, Arthur J. 75, 97
Powell, Alfred 122–4, 130
Scott, G.G. 13, 55
Shaw, R. Norman 7, 8, 36, 51, 53, 55, 95, 104, 105, 107
Shruffrey, L.A. 25
Street, G.E. 14, 51, 53–5, 56
Townsend, C. Harrison 8
Turner, Thackeray 8, 55–9, 122
Voysey, C.F.A. 8, 10, 53
Webb, Philip 8, 37–42, 51, 122

INDEX OF PLACES

ALFORD 111
ASH MANOR 77
BINSCOMBE 122
BETCHWORTH 36, 97
BLETCHINGLY 101
BRAMLEY 8, 104
14 *Snowdenham Hall*
CAPEL, *Oscrofts* 92
CHIDDINGFOLD 107
COMPTON 32, 66
CRANLEIGH 30, 31, 32
CROOKSBURY *House* 72–3, 80
Littleworth Cross 15
CROWHURST PLACE 12
DUNSFOLD 33
DUNSFOLD COMMON 31, 111
ELSTEAD, *Black Hams* 107
Fulbrook House 56, 67, 77, 125
EWHURST, *Coneyhurst* 122
Long Copse 122–4, 130
Marylands 123
Summersbury Farm 25, 27, 43
FARNCOMBE 78–9, 91
FARNHAM 8, 10, 36, 117, 119, 121
GODALMING 8, 9, 14, 25, 119, 121, 122
Orchards 8, 59–64, 65, 88, 125
Westbrook 55–9, 95, 96, 116, 122, 128
GODSTONE 82
GOMSHALL 29, 30, 78, 87
GREAT TANGLEY 12, 37–42, 82, 100, 104
GUILDFORD 14, 195, 119
Sutton Place 116
Abbots Hospital 128–9
HASLEMERE 78, 94, 122
Ballindune 88–9; *Hilders* 64, 75
Moses Hill Farm 25; *Valewood Farm* 113

HAWLANDS 128
HOLMBURY ST MARY
Holmwood 14, 53–5
LINGFIELD 12, *Old Guest House* 82, 100–4, 111
MERRIST WOOD 105, 107
MILFORD 105
MUNSTEAD WOOD 8–10, 83, 91, 125, 128–9, 138
NEWDIGATE 128, 136
NURSECOMBE BRAMLEY 27–8, 91
OAKWOOD PARK *Ruckmans* 70–2, 108
OCKHAM 98
OCKLEY 113; *Bonnets Farm* 78–9
Costers Farm 34; *Farm Place* 108
OXTED 122
PIRBRIGHT *Jerrys* 32
PUTTENDEN 128, 136
RAKE *House* 14, 43–8, 78
REDHILL *The Firs* 18;
Linkfield St. 111
SHERE 12, 51–2, 80, 112
SHOELANDS 77
SHOTTERMILL 77
THURSLEY 8, 91
TIGBOURNE COURT 79, 125–6
TILFORD *Tancreds Ford* 67–9, 121
VANN 33, 48–50, 60
WALTON-ON-THE-HILL 87, 117
Proffits Farm 86
WEST END *Lucas Green Manor* 92
WITLEY 113, *Pinewood* 14
WONERSH 112
WORPLESDON *Hurst Manor* 87

LIST OF ILLUSTRATIONS
(Entries for houses or cottages
unless otherwise stated)

	Page
ALFORD, shop and cottage	110
ASH MANOR, chimney detail	77
BETCHWORTH, *The Red Lion*	15
cottages	34
BLETCHINGLY, gable detail	104
BRAMLEY, half-timbering detail	104
CAPEL, Oscrofts	93
CHIDDINGFOLD	108
COMPTON	*plate i*
CRANLEIGH	30
CROOKSBURY HOUSE	73, 80
DUNSFOLD COMMON	31
Field Place	*plate iv*
EASHING	76
ELSTEAD, Black Hams Cottage	107
Fulbrook House	*plates ix, x*
Fulbrook stable, wall detail	125
EWHURST, gable detail	114
Long Copse	123, 124
Summersbury Farm	26
FARLEY GREEN, weatherboard detail	115
FARNCOMBE	78
chimney detail	91
FARNHAM, cottage near	11
view from Castle Keep	35
Beavers	118
Bridge Square	118
Longbridge House doorcase	120
Memorial Baths	120
Town Hall	119

LIST OF ILLUSTRATIONS

	Page
GODALMING, Church Street	96
High Street	97
cottage near the Station	116
Westbrook	57–8
GODSTONE, detail of roof construction	81
GOMSHALL	29, 88
chimney details	78, 79
GUILDFORD, High Street	94
door detail, Abbott's Hospital	128
HASLEMERE, Ballindune	89
Hilders	21
High Street	94
Moses Hill Farm	24
Old Fish Shop	*plate iii*
Valewood Farm	113
chimney detail	78
HOLMBURY ST. MARY, Holmwood	54–5
LINGFIELD, detail of shop	101
The Old Guest House	102–3
roof detail	81
MERRIST WOOD	106
MILFORD	106
MUNSTEAD WOOD	90
barns and garden	*plate ii*
gardener's cottage	9
door detail	128
NEWDIGATE, door detail	128
NURSECOMBE BRAMLEY	28, 90
OCKLEY	83
Bonnets Farm, chimney detail	80
Costers Farm	33
Farm Place	109
weather-tiling details	114
OCKHAM, barn at Mill Farm	99
ORCHARDS	60–3
OXTED, detail of glazing	135
PIRBRIGHT, Jerrys	32
PUTTENDEN, door detail	128
RAKE HOUSE	44–7
chimney detail	79

143

	Page
REDHILL, The Firs	19
Linkfield Street	112
RUCKMANS	71, 109
SHERE	52, 53
chimney detail	80
SHOELANDS, chimney detail	77
SHOTTERMILL, chimney detail	77
TIGBOURNE COURT	*frontispiece*
details of brickwork	*plates xiv, xv*
TILFORD, Tancreds Ford	*plates xi, xii*
UNSTEAD	74
VANN	*plates v–viii*
WALTON-ON-THE-HILL, Proffitts Farm	86
Inn, Chequers Lane	117
WEST END, Lucas Green Manor	92
WITLEY	*plate xvi*
Pinewood	13
weather-tile detail	114
WONERSH, chimney detail	80
WORPLESDON, Hurst Farm	87

*

cottage door designs	126, 128
PENTY: *Elements of Domestic Architecture:* dormers	98
eaves and guttering	99–100
fenestration	132–4
garage doors	129
latch	139
roof plans	84–6
weather-tiling, detail of 'kick'	110
examples of patterns	111
examples of shapes	112

Craddocks of Godalming, Great George Street, Godalming, Surrey